Brain Quest

Dear Parent,

"It's Fun to Be Smart!" That's not just our slogan, it's our philosophy. For fifteen years we've been adding a big dose of "fun" into learning—first with our bestselling Q&A Brain Quest card decks; then with all the licensed games and products bearing the Brain Quest brand; and now with BRAIN QUEST WORKBOOKS.

At Brain Quest we believe:

- All kids are smart—though they learn at their own speed.

- All kids learn best when they're having fun.

- All kids deserve the chance to reach their potential—given the tools they need, there's no limit to how far they can go!

BRAIN QUEST WORKBOOKS are the perfect tools to help children get a leg up in all areas of curriculum; they can hone their reading skills or dig in with math drills, review the basics or get a preview of lessons to come. These are not textbooks, but rather true workbooks—best used as supplements to what kids are learning in school, reinforcing curricular concepts while encouraging creative problem solving and higher-level thinking. You and your child can tackle a page or two a day—or an entire chapter over the course of a long holiday break. Your child will be getting great help with basic schoolwork, and you will be better able to gauge how well he or she is understanding course material.

Each BRAIN QUEST WORKBOOK has been written in consultation with an award-winning teacher specializing in that grade, and is compliant with most school curricula across the country. We cover the core competencies of reading, writing, and math in depth—with chapters on science, social studies, and other popular units rounding out the curriculum. Easy-to-navigate pages with color-coded tabs help identify chapters, while Brain Boxes offer parent-friendly explanations of key concepts and study units. That means parents can use the workbooks in conjunction with what their children are learning in school, or to explain material in ways that are consistent with current teaching strategies. In either case, the workbooks create an important bridge to the classroom, an effective tool for parents, homeschoolers, tutors, and teachers alike.

BRAIN QUEST WORKBOOKS all come with a variety of fun extras: a pull-out poster; Brain Quest "mini-cards" based on the bestselling Brain Quest game; two pages of stickers; and a Brainiac Award Certificate to celebrate successful completion of the workbook.

Learning is an adventure—a quest for knowledge. At Brain Quest we strive to guide children on that quest, to keep them motivated and curious, and to give them the confidence they need to do well in school . . . and beyond. We're confident that BRAIN QUEST WORKBOOKS will play an integral role in your child's adventure. So let the learning—and the fun—begin!

—The editors of Brain Quest

This book belongs to:

_____

Library of Congress Cataloging-in-Publication Data is available.

ISBN 978-0-7611-4914-9

Workbook series design by Raquel Jaramillo
Illustrations by Stephen Lewis and Kimble Mead

Workman books are available at special discounts when purchased in bulk for premiums and sales promotions as well as for fund-raising or educational use. Special editions or book excerpts also can be created to specification. For details, contact the Special Sales Director at the address below or send an email to specialmarkets@workman.com.

Workman Publishing Co., Inc.
225 Varick Street
New York, NY 10014-4381
workman.com

Printed in the United States of America
First printing June 2008

51 50 49 48

Brain Quest Grade 1 Workbook

Written by Lisa Trumbauer
Consulting Editor: Betsy Rogers

WORKMAN PUBLISHING
NEW YORK

4

Contents

Phonics

Super Safari!

The names of these animals all start with the **b, d,** or **f** sound.
Say the word for each animal.
What beginning sound do you hear?
Write the letter.

dog

eer

Brain Box

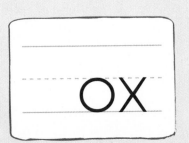

ox

A **consonant** is any
letter in the alphabet
that is not a vowel.

at

ly

rog

ear

uck

eaver

To the Castle!

The things in this picture all start with the **h, j, k,** or **q** sound.

Say the word for each picture.

What beginning sound do you hear?

Write the letter.

arp

at

ar

itten

uilt

ueen

ing

ester

Monster Manor!

The things in this picture all start with the **l, m, n,** or **p** sound.

Say the word for each picture.

What beginning sound do you hear?

Write the letter.

et

onkey

uzzle

onster

izard

oon

ollipop

oodles

izza

Blast Off!

Phonics

Beginning consonants

The things in this picture all start with the **r, s,** or **t** sound.
Say the word for each picture.
What beginning sound do you hear?
Write the letter.

___urtle

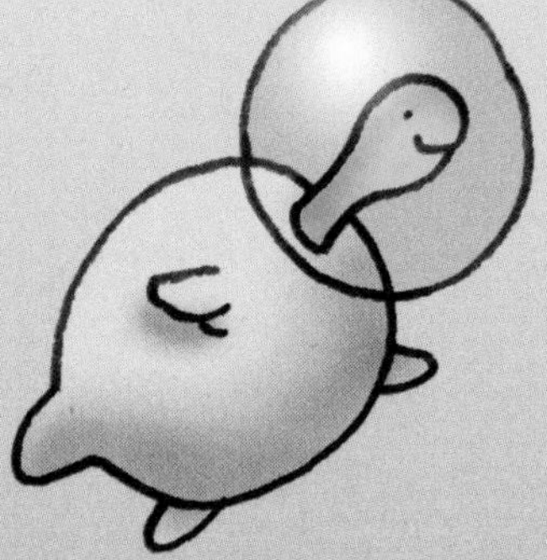

___eal

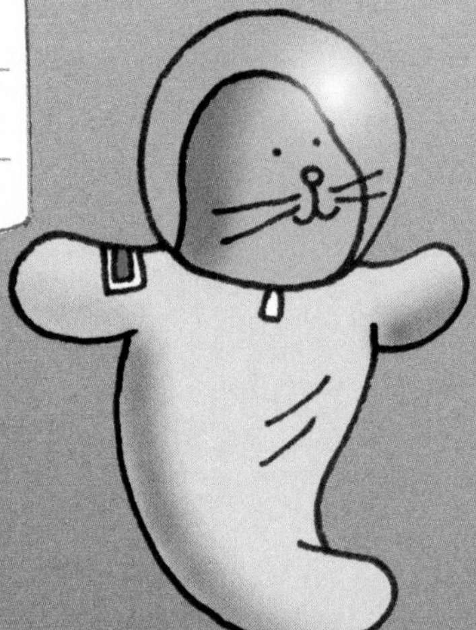

___ocket

___nake

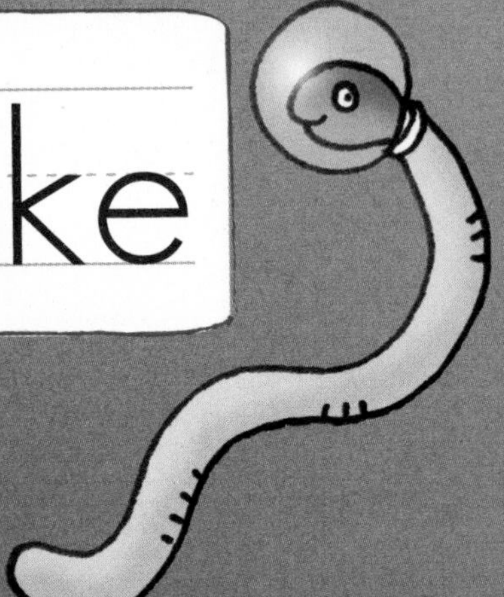

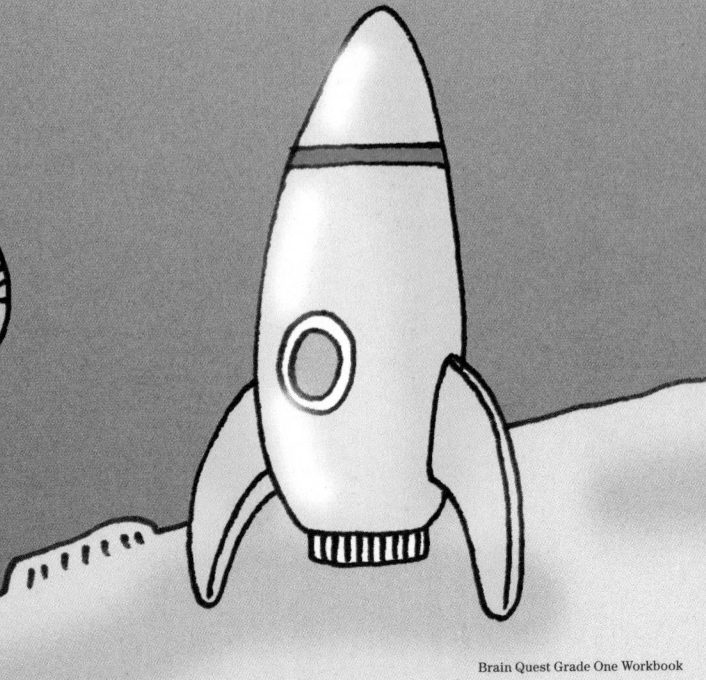

accoon

iger

abbit

elescope

Wacky Wizard!

The things in this picture all start with the
v, w, x, y, or **z** sound.
Say the word for each picture.
What beginning sound do you hear?
Write the letter.

Phonics

Beginning
consonants

ase

o-yo

histle

acuum

izard

ebra

ipper

arn

-ray

City and Country

Say the word for each picture.

If you hear a **hard c** sound, draw a line to the **country.**

If you hear a **soft c** sound, draw a line to the **city.**

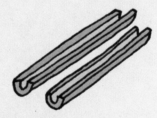

Brain Box

The letter **c** has two sounds: a **hard c** sound as in **country** and a **soft c** sound as in **city.**

Girl and Giant

Say the word for each picture.

If you hear a **hard g** sound, draw a line to the **girl**.

If you hear a **soft g** sound, draw a line to the **giant**.

giant

girl

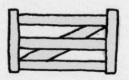

Brain Box

The letter **g** has two sounds: a **hard g** sound as in **girl** and a **soft g** sound as in **giant**.

Web and Kid

The words for these pictures all end in **b** or **d**.
Say the word for each picture.
What ending sound do you hear?
Write the letter.

bir

brea

cri

ki

cra

sle

we

bi

Sun and Swim

The things in this picture all end in **m** or **n**.
Say the word for each thing in the picture.
What ending sound do you hear?
Write the letter.

Phonics

Ending consonants

su

fa

swi

ma

pe

cla

dru

Ship and Boat

The words for these pictures all end in **p** or **t**.
Say the word for each picture.
What ending sound do you hear?
Write the letter.

Phonics

Ending
consonants

shi

boa

ne

boo

ma

peanu

po

shee

Snail and Bus

The words for these pictures all end in
l or **ll**, **s** or **ss**.

Say the word for each picture.

What ending sound do you hear?

Write the letter.

snai

bu

ba

gla

do

dre

she

plu

Phonics

Ending
consonants

Brain Quest Grade One Workbook

Frog and Duck

The words for these pictures all end in **g** or **k**.
Say the word for each picture.
Circle the pictures that end with a **g** sound.
Underline the pictures that end with a **k** sound.

Chicken Checkers!

Say the word for each picture.

Circle the pictures that begin with the **ch** sound.

Brain Box

Sometimes two consonants that are next to each other make a new sound.

Example: **chip**

When you say **chip,** you don't hear the **c** and **h** sounds separately. You hear the new **ch** sound.

Show Me!

Say the word for each picture.
Circle the pictures that begin with
the **sh** sound.

Brain Box

Sometimes two consonants that are next to each
other make a new sound.

Example: **shovel**

When you say **shovel**, you don't hear the **s** and **h**
sounds separately. You hear the new **sh** sound.

The Theater!

Say the word for each picture.
Circle the pictures that begin with
the **th** sound.

Brain Box

Sometimes two consonants that are next to each
other make a new sound.

Example: **theater**

When you say **theater,** you don't hear the **t** and
h sounds separately. You hear the new **th** sound.

Short a

Say the word for each picture.
Color the cards with pictures that have
the **short a** sound.

Phonics

Short vowel
sounds

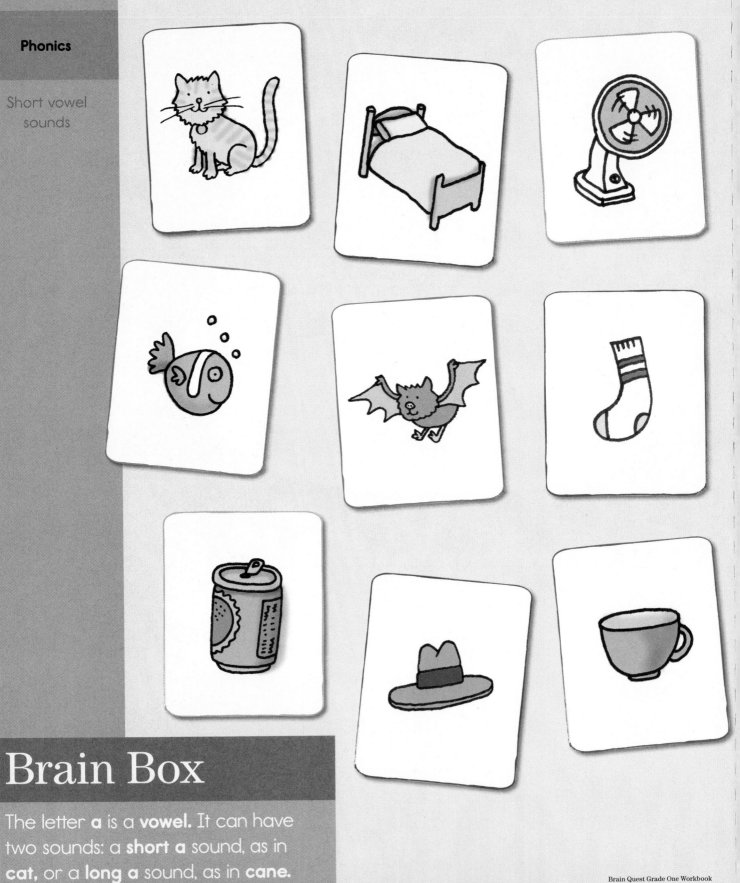

Brain Box

The letter **a** is a **vowel.** It can have
two sounds: a **short a** sound, as in
cat, or a **long a** sound, as in **cane.**

Short e

Say the word for each picture.
Color the cards with pictures that have
the **short e** sound.

Brain Box

The letter **e** is a **vowel**. It can have
two sounds: a **short e** sound, as in
bed, or a **long e** sound, as in **bee**.

Short i

Say the word for each picture.
Color the cards with pictures that have
the **short i** sound.

Phonics

Short vowel
sounds

Brain Box

The letter **i** is a **vowel.** It can have
two sounds: a **short i** sound, as in
fish, or a **long i** sound, as in **bike.**

Short o

Say the word for each picture.
Color the cards with pictures that have
the **short o** sound.

Brain Box

The letter **o** is a **vowel.** It can have
two sounds: a **short o** sound, as in
mop, or a **long o** sound, as in **yo-yo.**

Short u

Say the word for each picture.
Color the cards with pictures that have
the **short u** sound.

Brain Box

The letter **u** is a **vowel.** It can have
two sounds: a **short u** sound, as in
sun, or a **long u** sound, as in **blue.**

Long a

Say the word for each picture.
Color the cards with pictures that have
the **long a** sound.

Brain Box

The letter **a** is a **vowel.** It can have
two sounds: a **short a** sound, as in
cat, or a **long a** sound, as in **cane.**

32

Long e

Say the word for each picture.
Color the cards with pictures that have
the **long e** sound.

Brain Box

The letter **e** is a **vowel.** It can have
two sounds: a **short e** sound, as in
bed, or a **long e** sound, as in **bee.**

Long i

Say the word for each picture.
Color the cards with pictures that have
the **long i** sound.

Brain Box

The letter **i** is a **vowel.** It can have
two sounds: a **short i** sound, as in
fish, or a **long i** sound, as in **bike.**

Long o

Say the word for each picture.
Color the cards with pictures that have
the **long o** sound.

Brain Box

The letter **o** is a **vowel.** It can have
two sounds: a **short o** sound, as in
mop, or a **long o** sound, as in **yo-yo.**

Long u

Say the word for each picture.
Color the cards with pictures that have
the **long u** sound.

Brain Box

The letter **u** is a **vowel.** It can have
two sounds: a **short u** sound, as in
sun, or a **long u** sound, as in **blue.**

Long Vowel Review

Circle the word that has the same long vowel sound as the first word.

| float | ox | (hope) | read |

| hike | cube | big | like |

| brain | lane | seem | bat |

| queen | pen | look | heel |

| flew | but | shoe | flea |

Cat and Snake

Say the word for each picture.

Draw a line from the pictures with the **short a** sound to the **cat.**

Draw a line from the pictures with the **long a** sound to the **snake.**

cat

snake

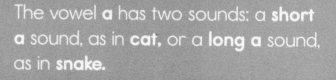

Brain Box

The vowel **a** has two sounds: a **short a** sound, as in **cat,** or a **long a** sound, as in **snake.**

Red and Green

Say the word for each picture.

Draw a line from the pictures with the **short e** sound to the **red** splash.

Draw a line from the pictures with the **long e** sound to the **green** splash.

red   green

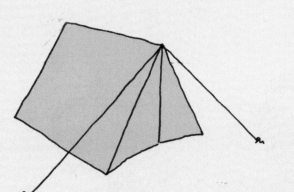

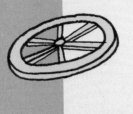

Brain Box

The vowel **e** has two sounds: a **short e** sound, as in **red**, or a **long e** sound, as in **green**.

Jill and Mike

Say the word for each picture.

Draw a line from the pictures with the **short i** sound to **Jill.**

Draw a line from the pictures with the **long i** sound to **Mike.**

Jill

Mike

9

Brain Box

The vowel **i** has two sounds: a **short i** sound, as in **Jill,** or a **long i** sound, as in **Mike.**

Fox and Goat

Say the word for each picture.

Draw a line from the pictures with the **short o** sound to the **fox.**

Draw a line from the pictures with the **long o** sound to the **goat.**

fox

goat

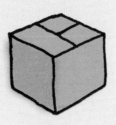

Brain Box

The vowel **o** has two sounds: a **short o** sound, as in **fox,** or a **long o** sound, as in **goat.**

Sun and Moon

Say the word for each picture.

Draw a line from the pictures with the **short u** sound to the **sun**.

Draw a line from the pictures with the **long u** sound to the **moon**.

sun

moon

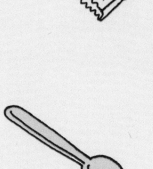

Brain Box

The vowel **u** has two sounds: a **short u** sound, as in **sun,** or a **long u** sound, as in **moon.**

Spy and Lady

Say the word for each picture.

Draw a line from the pictures that end
with the **long i** sound to the **spy.**

Draw a line from the pictures that end
with the **long e** sound to the **lady.**

spy

lady

Brain Box

The letter **y** can have two sounds:
a **long i** sound, as in **spy,** or a
long e sound, as in **lady.**

Spelling

Pets! Pets! Pets!

Say the name for each animal.
Write the first letter to complete each word.

Spelling

Beginning
letters

___ og

___ nake

___ at

___ rog

ird

ig

abbit

izard

urtle

In the Tree House

Say each word.
What **short vowel** sound do you hear?
Write the vowel to complete each word.

Spelling

Short vowels

sh_p

m_p

d_ll

pl_nt

w   b

st   ck

cl   ck

r   g

b   ll

be

lam

do

cor

Shipshape!

Complete each sentence with a **long a** word from the Word Box.

wave	sail	nail
whale	chain	cake

The _____ swims

in the ocean.

Patchy hammers a

_____ .

Curly eats a piece of

_____ .

The anchor is on

a _____ .

Squirt sews the

hole in the _____ .

The _____

splashes onto the ship.

Spelling

Long a words

Brain Box

Long a words can be spelled in different ways.

Some long a words are spelled with ai, as in rain.

Some long a words are spelled with a_e, as in rake.

Trees and Leaves

Complete each sentence with a **long e** word from the Word Box.

queen	bee	wheel
peach	feet	seal

Watch out! That  _____ might sting you.

I have ten toes on my _____ .

Brain Box

Long e words can be spelled in different ways.

Some **long e** words are spelled with **ee**, as in **tree**.

Some **long e** words are spelled with **ea**, as in **leaf**.

The  _____

plays in the waves.

My favorite dessert is _____ pie.

The _____

wears a crown.

The _____

goes round and round.

Spelling

Long e words

A Day at the Park

Complete each sentence with a **long i** word from the Word Box.

bike	fly	pie
sky	tie	slide

Brain Box

Long **i** words can be spelled in different ways.

Some **long i** words are spelled with **i_e**, as in **mice**.

Some **long i** words are spelled with **ie**, as in **lie**.

And other **long i** words are spelled with **y**, as in **cry**.

Amy rides a _____ .

Lori goes down the
_____
_____ .

Rico eats the _____ .

Cody wears a _____ .

There are no clouds in
the _____ .

The _____ is buzzing
around.

Backyard Barbecue

Complete each sentence with a **long o** word from the Word Box.

toad	smoke	bone
cone	hose	boat

The kids are holding the

_____ .

A fire makes _____ .

Mom eats an ice-cream

_____ .

The dog has a _____ .

The _____ jumps

into the pool.

A _____ floats

in the water.

Brain Box

Long o words can be spelled in different ways.

Some long o words are spelled with o_e, as in nose.

Some long o words are spelled with oa, as in goat.

Dude Ranch

Complete each sentence with a **long u** word from the Word Box.

mule	stool	tune
room	tooth	boots

The cowboy _____ are blue.

Billy hums a _____ .

The _____ can carry a heavy load.

The horse's big _____ sticks out of his mouth.

Ramón stands on a _____ .

There are two horses in the _____ .

Brain Box

Long u words can be spelled in different ways.

Some **long u** words are spelled with **u_e,** as in **dude.**

Some **long u** words are spelled with **oo,** as in **moon.**

Word Builders

Complete each word with a **blend** from the Word Box.

tr	fr	cr
br	gr	dr

_____ oom

_____ ab

_____ og

_____ uck

_____ ape

_____ um

Brain Box

Blends are two consonants that go together. You can hear both letters in a blend.

Example: **drum**

Drum has an **r-blend.** When you say **drum,** you can hear both the **d** and the **r** sounds.

Slip and Slide

Complete each word with a **blend** from the Word Box.

pl	gl	bl
sl	cl	pl

 _____ide

 _____ane

 _____ack

 _____ant

 _____ass

 _____over

Brain Box

Blends are two consonants that go together. You can hear both letters in a blend.

Example: **plane**

Plane has an **l-blend.** When you say **plane**, you can hear both the **p** and the **l** sounds.

Super S

Complete each word with a **blend** from the Word Box.

Spelling

s-blends

sn	sk	sp
sw	st	sm

_____ ail

_____ ar

_____ ate

_____ iral

_____ ing

_____ ile

Brain Box

Blends are two consonants that go together. You can hear both letters in a blend.

Example: **snap**

Snap has an **s-blend.** When you say **snap,** you can hear both the **s** and the **n** sounds.

Vocabulary

All About Mike

Read the words on the cards.
Write each word in the correct sentence.

am

and

I

you

I _____ Mike!

_____ like to read _____
play.

What do _____ like
to do?

is

run

see

my

This is _____ dog!

His name _____ Rex.

He likes to _____ .

He must _____ a squirrel.

Where Is Everyone?

Read the words on the cards.
Write each word in the correct sentence.

Where is the boy?

_______ is on the swing.

Where is the girl?

_______ is on the slide.

Where is the ball?

_______ is under the tree.

Where are the twins?

_______ are on the seesaw.

Vocabulary

Sight words

Team Up

Read the words on the cards.
Write each word in the correct sentence.

His   Their

Her   Its

These are the Tigers.

They are a team.

_____
_____ shirts are red.

This is Sue.

_____
_____ shirt is orange.

This is Jack.

_____
_____ shirt is green.

This is the mascot.

_____
_____ fur is striped.

On the Farm

Read the words on the cards.
Write each word next to the correct animal.

Vocabulary

Animal words

cat

dog

cow

hen

horse   goat   duck   pig

In the Kitchen

Read the words on the cards.

Draw a line from each card to the correct picture on the next page.

bowl

pot

cup

spoon

sink

pan

A Day at the Beach

Read the words on the cards.

Draw a line from each card to the correct picture on the next page.

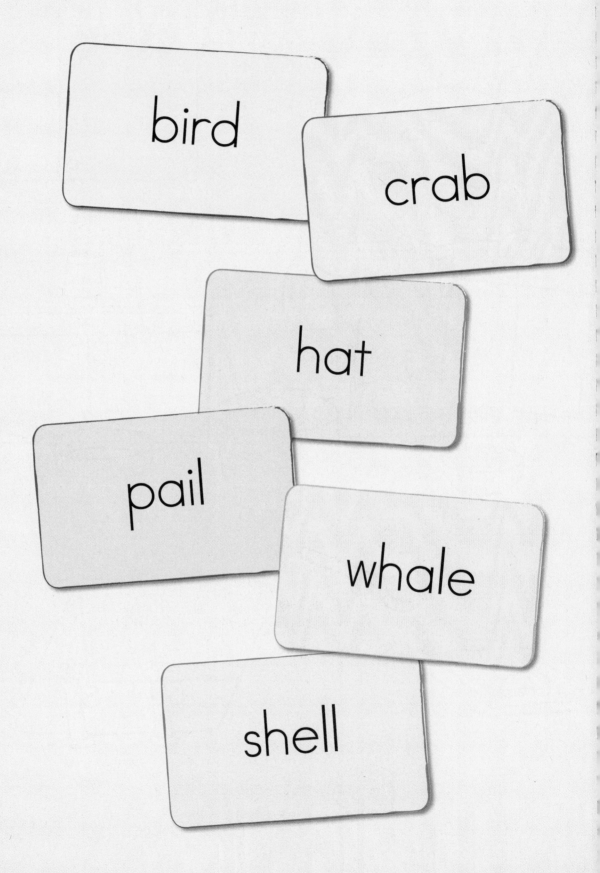

bird

crab

hat

pail

whale

shell

Vocabulary

Beach words

Picnic Party

Read the words on the cards.
Draw a line from each card to the correct picture on the next page.

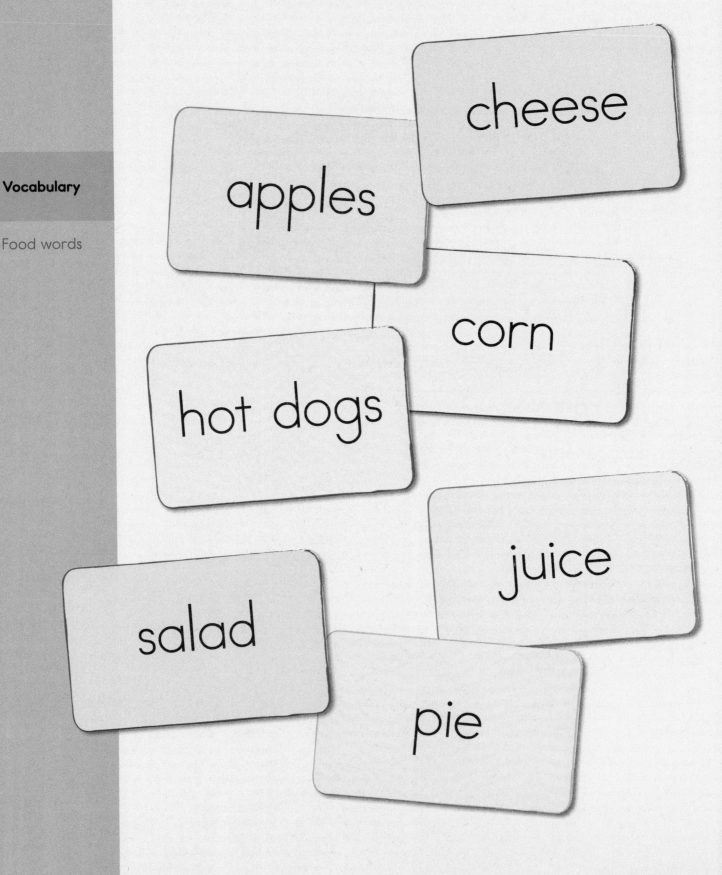

cheese

apples

corn

hot dogs

juice

salad

pie

Teatime!

Look at the picture.
Read the words on the cards.
Write each word in the correct sentence.

Vocabulary

Tea words

The animals sit on

_____

- - - - - - - - - - - -

_____ .

The mouse carries his

_____

- - - - - - - - - -

_____ .

The _____ is pink.

The rabbit tastes the

_____

- - - - - - - - - -

_____ .

Color Splash!

Read the color words on the cards.
Color the card the right color.

Vocabulary

Color words

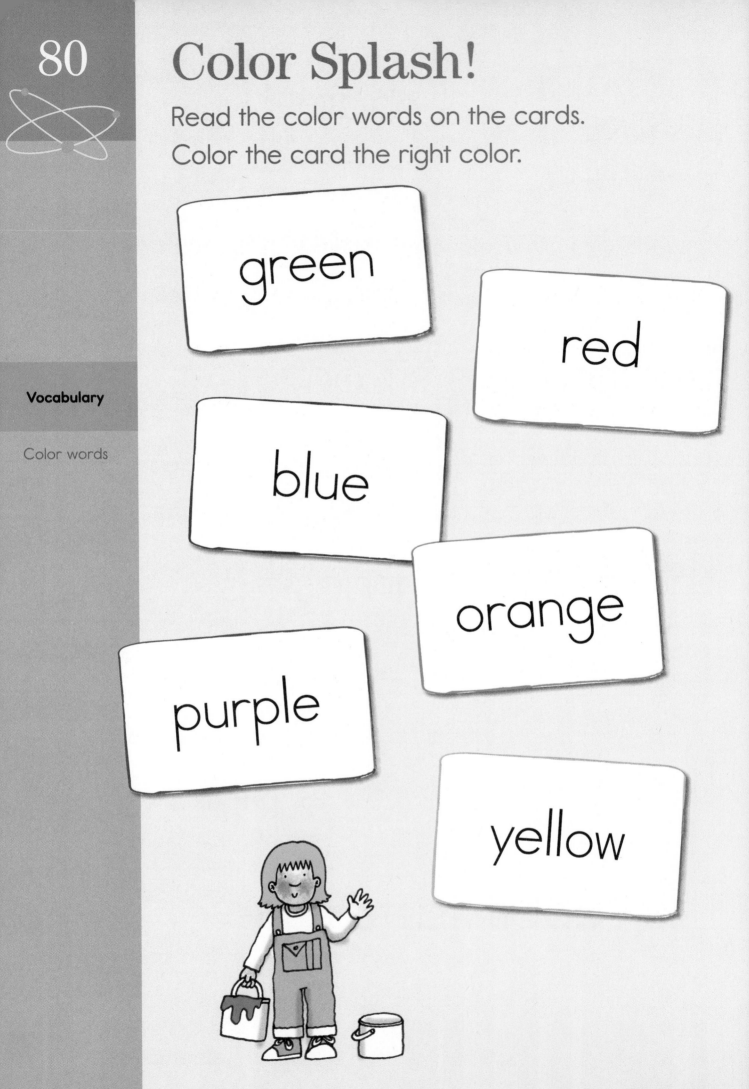

green

red

blue

orange

purple

yellow

Write the color word below each color.

_____

_ _ _ _ _ _ _ _ _ _ _ _ _

_____

_____

_ _ _ _ _ _ _ _ _ _ _ _ _

_____

_____

_ _ _ _ _ _ _ _ _ _ _ _ _

_____

Finger Counting

Read the number words on the cards.

Count the number of fingers
each hand is holding up.

Draw a line from each card to the
correct hand.

two

four

one

five

three

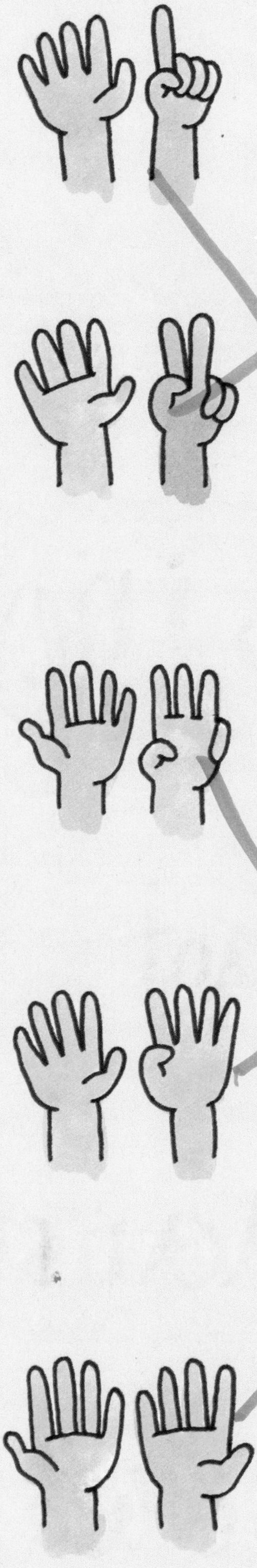

seven

nine

six

ten

eight

Activities!

Read the words on the cards.

Write each word in the correct sentence.

| dance | paint | sing | read |

Vocabulary

Action words

I like to ___sing___.

I like to ___pant___

We like to ___dance___.

I like to ___read___

Soccer Stars!

Read the words on the cards.
Write each word in the correct sentence.

catch | kick | cheer | jog

We _jog_ .

We _kick_ .

We _catch_ .

We _cheer_ .

Let's Go!

Read the words on the cards.

Write each word next to the correct picture.

bike

bus

boat

car

car

boat

bike

bus

plane   train   truck   van

plane

truck

train

van

Time to Rhyme!

The words on the cards all rhyme with **brag** .
Write each rhyming word next
to the correct picture.

Vocabulary

Rhyming
words

tag
wag
bag
flag

tag   bag

flag

wag

Brain Box

Rhyming words have
the same middle and
ending sounds.
Cat and **hat** are
rhyming words.

The words on the cards all rhyme with **tan** .
Write each rhyming word next
to the correct picture.

can

pan

man

fan

Vocabulary

Rhyming
words

man

fan

can

pan

Keep Rhyming!

The words on the cards all rhyme with **cool**.
Write each rhyming word under
the correct picture.

stool   school   spool   pool

Vocabulary

Rhyming
words

The words on the cards all rhyme with **tone** .
Write each rhyming word under
the correct picture.

bone phone stone cone

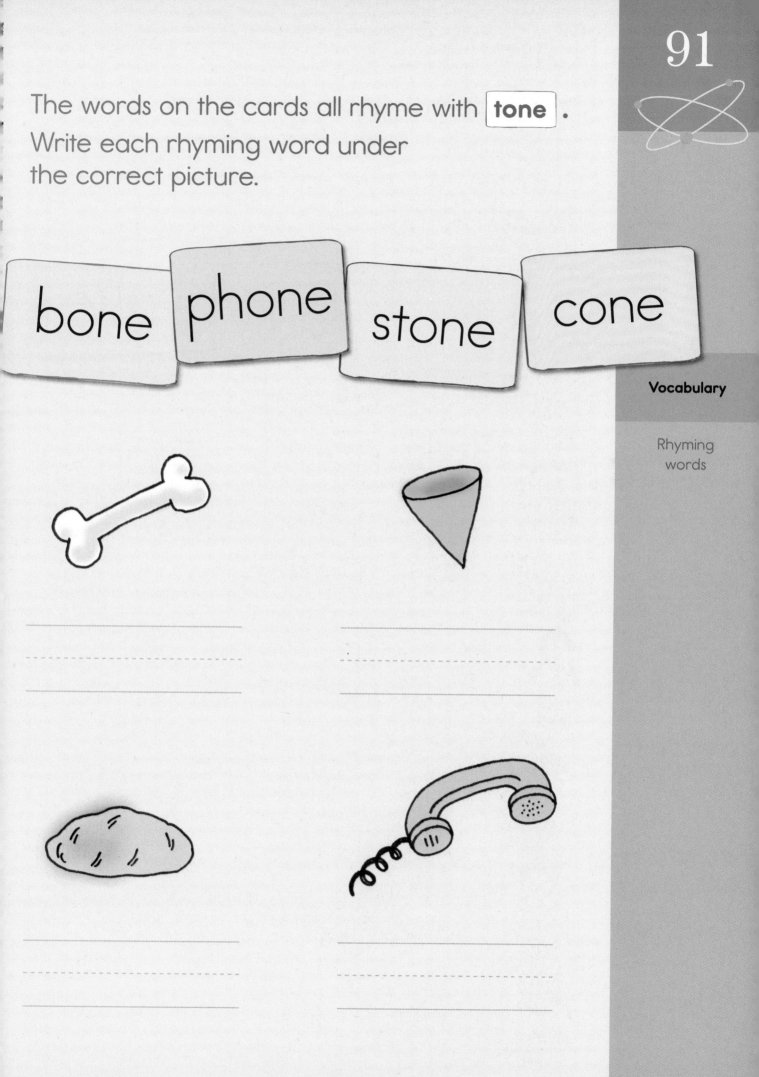

_____

_____

_____

_____

_____

_____

_____

_____

Our Pets

The words on the cards are the pet names.
Each pet's name rhymes with its owner's name.
Complete each sentence with the correct
rhyming pet name.

Nate   Harry   Spike

My name is Larry.

My dog is _____ .

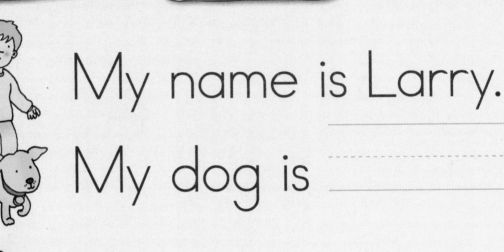

My name is Kate.

My cat is _____ .

My name is Mike.

My dog is _____

My name is Hailey.
My dog is _____ .

Vocabulary

Rhyming words

My name is Andy.
My cat is _____ .

My name is Jan.
My cat is _____ .

Find the Rhyme

Say the word for each picture.
Draw a line from each picture to
the word it rhymes with.

vest

junk

feel

main

rice

Language Arts

People

Read the **nouns** in the Word Box.
They all name people.
Complete each sentence with the correct
noun from the Word Box.

| daughter | boy | woman | father | veterinarian |

Brain Box

A **noun** is a word
that names a person,
place, or thing.

The _____ examines the cat.

The _____ is wearing a brown sweater.

His _____ has pigtails.

The _____ has red hair.

The _____ has a birdcage.

Animals

Read the **nouns** in the Word Box.
They all name animals.

turtle	cat	bird	dog

Brain Box

Animal words are

nouns.

Complete each sentence with the correct **noun** from the Word Box.

The _____ chirps on a branch.

The _____ hides behind the bush.

The _____ walks on a leash.

The _____ rests on the rock.

Things

Read the **nouns** in the Word Box.
They all name things.

hammer	nails	saw	wood

Complete each sentence with the correct **noun** from the Word Box.

José wants to build a birdhouse.

He has planks of

_____

_____ .

He has a _____ to cut the wood.

He has a box of

_____

_____ .

The _____ is next to his sister.

Places

Read the **nouns** in the Word Box.
They all name places.

beach	city	farm
forest	lake	town

Brain Box

Words for places are
nouns.

103

Complete each sentence with the correct **noun** from the Word Box.

The cow lives on the

_____ .

The _____ has trees.

The boat floats on the

_____ .

There are tall buildings

in the _____ .

There is sand on the

_____ .

We drive into _____ .

Go, Dino, Go!

Circle the **verb** in each sentence.

The dinosaur eats.

The dinosaur hops.

The dinosaur runs.

Brain Box

A **verb** is an action word. A **verb** tells what someone or something does

Example: The dinosaur **sings.**

In this sentence, **sings** is the **verb.** It tells what the dinosaur does.

The dinosaur hugs.

The dinosaur sleeps.

The dinosaur waves.

Describe It!

Read the **adjectives** in the Word Boxes.
Write the correct **adjective** to tell about each
alien from outer space.

happy	sad	wide

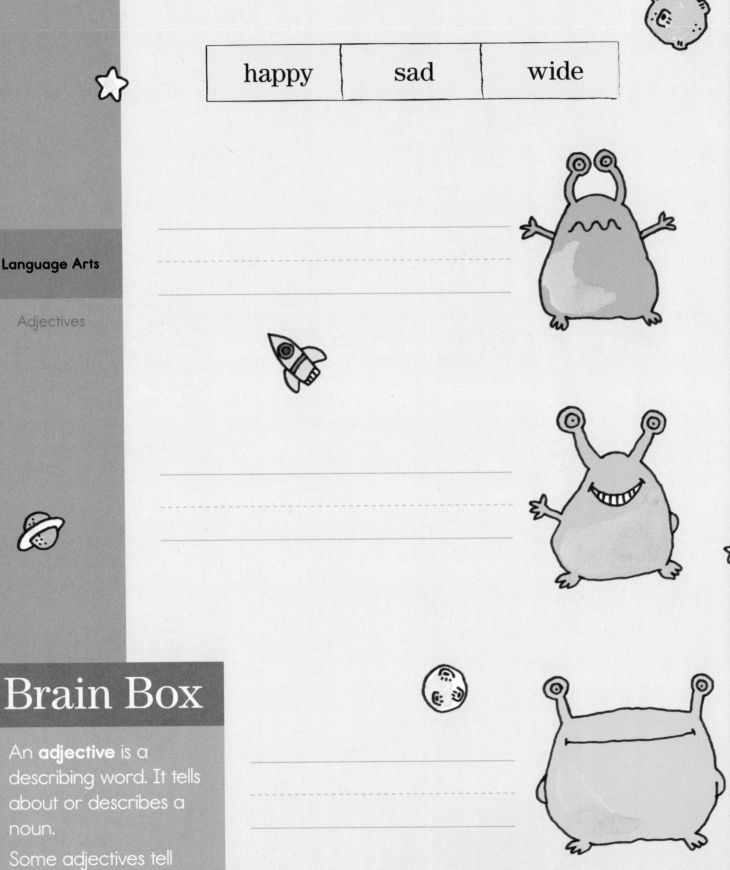

_____

_____

_____

Language Arts

Adjectives

Brain Box

An **adjective** is a
describing word. It tells
about or describes a
noun.

Some adjectives tell
what nouns look like.

| curly | tall | small |

Describe It!

Read the **adjectives** in the Word Boxes.
Write the correct **adjective** to tell about each animal.

white	green	gray

The _____ elephant lives in Africa.

The _____ polar bear lives in the arctic.

The _____ lizard lives in the desert.

| pink | brown | red |

The _____ flamingo lives near the water.

The _____ kangaroo lives in Australia.

The _____ deer lives in the forest.

Brain Box

Color words are **adjectives.** Color words tell what things look like.

Cat Chase!

Read this **sentence:**

The cat naps.

Circle the **noun.**

Underline the **verb.**

Draw a box around the **capital letter** that begins the sentence.

Draw a triangle around the **period** that ends the sentence.

Now copy the **sentence** here.

_____

- - - - - - - - - - - - - - - - - - -

_____

Language Arts

Statements

Brain Box

A **sentence** is a group of words that express a complete thought.

All sentences begin with a capital letter.

A **statement** is a sentence that explains or tells what someone or something does.

A **statement** ends with a period.

Circle the **noun** in this sentence:

The cat wakes up.

Underline the **verb** in this sentence:

The cat runs.

Draw a box around the **capital letter** that begins this sentence:

The dog chases the cat.

Draw a triangle around the **period** that ends this sentence:

The dog naps.

Superstar!

These sentences are written wrong.
Write each sentence correctly.

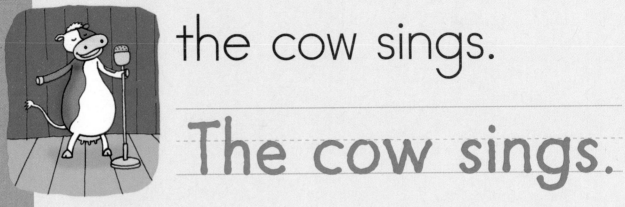

the cow sings.

The cow sings.

Language Arts

Statements

the cow dances

_____

the cow acts

_____

Brain Box

A **statement** begins
with a capital letter.
A **statement** ends with
a period.

The receives cow flowers.

_____

- -

_____

cow bows. The

_____

- -

_____

waves the cow

_____

- -

_____

So Many Questions!

These questions are written wrong.
Write each sentence correctly.

how do you feel

_____

_____

who is your best friend

_____

_____

when is your next show

_____

_____

what is your favorite song

_____

_____

_____

Brain Box

Some sentences ask
a **question.**
A **question** begins
with a capital letter.
A **question** ends with
a question mark.

More Dessert, Please?

Read each **question.**
Circle the question word.

What kind of
dessert is it?

Who made
the dessert?

Where is the dessert?

When was the
dessert ready?

Why did they make
the dessert?

How does it taste?

Language Arts

Question
words

Brain Box

Questions start with
question words.

**Who, what, where,
when, why,** and **how**
are all question words.

She Makes Pizza

Add the letter **s** to each verb to tell what is happening now.

She roll___ out the pizza dough.

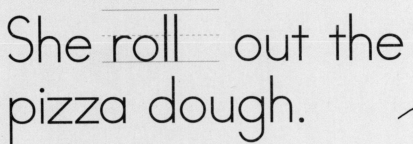

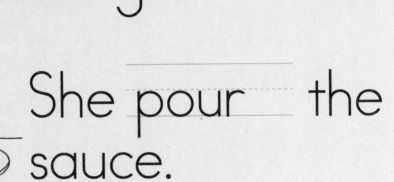

She pour___ the sauce.

She sprinkle___ the cheese.

She put___ the pizza in the oven.

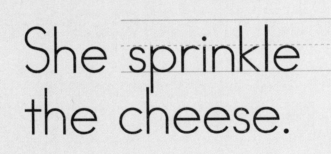

Brain Box

A **present-tense verb** tells what is happening now.
You can add the letter **s** to many verbs to tell about what is happening now.

She take___ out the pizza.

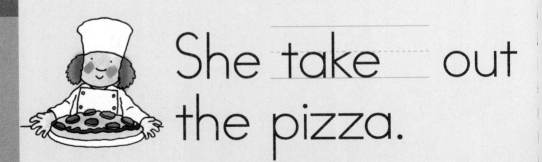

They Made a Sundae!

Add the letters **ed** to tell what happened in the past.

He scoop____ the ice cream.

She pour____ the sauce.

He add____ the bananas.

She spoon____ the nuts.

He look____ at the sundae.

Brain Quest Grade One Workbook

Language Arts

Past-tense verbs

Brain Box

A **past-tense verb** tells what happened in the past.

You can add **ed** to many verbs to tell about actions that happened in the past.

The More the Merrier!

Look at the picture. Complete each sentence using the word **is** or **are**.

The monkeys _____ climbing.

The elephant _____ spraying.

The lions _____ roaring.

The giraffe _____ eating.

The zebra _____ dancing.

The hippos _____ singing.

Farmer's Market

Write the plural for each food word by adding the letter **s** at the end of the word.

pumpkin

pumpkins

pepper

_____

carrot

_____

apple

_____

Brain Box

Plural means there is more than one.

You can add an **s** to make most nouns plural.

Reading

Drake the Dragon

Read about Drake.
Then answer the questions.

Reading

Comprehension

This is Drake.

Drake is a dragon.

Drake is purple.

Drake lives in a cave.

Drake lives with a snake.

Drake and the snake are best friends.

What is Drake?

Drake is a **dragon** .

What color is Drake?

Drake is _____ .

Where does
Drake live?

Drake lives in a

_____

_____ .

Who is Drake's
best friend?

Drake's best friend is a

_____

_____ .

Picking Apples

Read about apples.
Then answer the questions.

Apples grow on trees.

You can pick apples in the fall.

This family is picking red apples.

Where do apples grow?
Apples grow on

_____

_____ .

When can you pick apples?
You can pick apples in the _____ .

What color are the apples on the trees?
The apples are

_____

_____ .

Camp Out

Read about the camping trip.

Number the pictures from 1 to 4 to show what happens in order.

1. We find a spot by the river.

2. We set up our tents.

3. We get some sticks for a fire.

4. We make dinner and sing!

Robot Race

Read about Robbie.
Then answer the questions.

Reading

Comprehension

Robbie is a robot.

Robbie is in a race.

Robbie has wheels for feet!

Robbie rolls fast.

He rolls past the other robots.

Robbie wins the race!

What is Robbie?

Robbie is a _____ .

What does Robbie have for feet?

Robbie has _____ .

Who wins the race?

_____

_____

wins the race.

Draw your own robot here!

A Big Day

Read the sentences.

Choose the correct feeling word to tell how each person feels. Write it on the line.

Mario can't wait to get to the zoo.

Mario is _____ .

excited	angry

Reading

Making inferences

Kate's kite is stuck in a tree!

Kate is _____ .

upset	happy

Steve doesn't know anyone at the party.

Steve is _____

silly	shy

Marty is _____ .

| sad | sleepy |

Marty lost
his dog.

Marty is _____ .

| mad | glad |

Marty found
his dog!

Luis is _____ .

| tired | frightened |

Luis played a
long game
of baseball.

Plants!

Read about plants.

Flowers are plants.

Trees are plants.

Grass is a plant, too.

Rocks are not plants.

Water is not a plant.

The rabbit is not a plant.

Color the cards with plant words green.

rocks

rabbit

trees

grass

flowers

water

Allie the Alien

Read about Allie.

Reading

Prior
knowledge

Allie has strong eyes.

Allie sees lots of things on Earth.

She sees land.

She sees water.

She sees animals.

Allie sees you, too!

What does Allie see on Earth? Write it on the lines.

She sees land.

Send a postcard to Allie.
Draw a picture of yourself saying hello!

Monster Music!

Read each sentence.
Then draw a line to the matching picture.

Reading

Comprehension

Molly plays
the drums.

Michael
plays the
tuba.

Mark plays
the violin.

Maria plays
the flute.

If you were a monster, what would you play?

I would play the

_____

Draw yourself playing your instrument.

Reading

Comprehension

The Witch's Spell

Read about the witch.
Number the pictures from 1 to 5 to
show what happens in order.

1. Wilma the Witch has a frog.

2. She turns the frog into a bird!

3. She turns the bird into a bug!

4. She turns the bug into a dog!

5. She turns the dog into a frog again.

Reading

Sequencing

Duck's Day

Read about Duck.

Duck went for a walk.

It was a sunny day.

Duck felt a drop.

It began to rain!

That was okay.

Duck liked the rain.

Reading

Predicting

What do you predict Duck will do in the rain?
Draw a picture!

Writing

Doggy Diary

Complete each sentence with a word
from the Word Box.

Then copy the whole sentence on the blank.

| bark | happy | stick | Gus | fetch |

My name is _____.

_____

_____

I like to _____.

_____

_____

Writing

Sentence
construction

I fetch a _____ .

 I like to _____ .

I am a _____ dog.

All About You!

Complete each sentence with a word that tells about you. Then copy the whole sentence on the blank.

My name is _____ .

_____

_____

I like the color _____ .

_____

_____

My favorite animal is
a/an _____ .

_____

_____

Writing

Sentence construction

Now draw a picture of yourself wearing your favorite color and playing with your favorite animal.

Writing

Sentence
construction

Playing at the Pond

Write a sentence about each animal you see at the pond. Begin each sentence with **I see a.**

frog

fox

duck

I see a duck.

deer

fish

turtle

Brain Box

A **statement** is a sentence that explains or tells what someone or something does.

A statement begins with a capital letter and ends with a period.

Writing

Statements

Let's Ride!

Write a sentence about each way to ride.

Begin each sentence with **I ride in a.**

boat

car

I ride in a car.

plane

train

wagon

Silly Pig!

Complete each sentence with the correct word from the Word Box.

Copy the whole sentence on the blank.

silly	sad	angry

The pig is _____

_____

_____

house	tree	mud

The pig rolls in _____

_____

_____

runs	dances	sits

The pig _____

_____

Brain Quest Grade One Workbook

Writing

Sentence construction

eats	sleeps	sings

The pig _____ .

dog	cat	girl

The pig likes the _____ .

ice cream	pizza	cookies

They eat _____ .

Writing

Sentence construction

Grandma's House

Write three sentences that tell what is happening at Grandma's house.

First, choose a **noun.**

Second, choose a **verb.**

Now write a sentence using both words.

Your sentence should start with the word **The.**

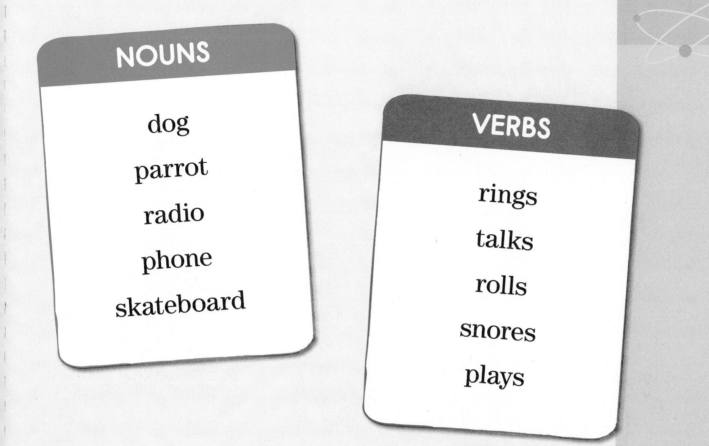

NOUNS

dog

parrot

radio

phone

skateboard

VERBS

rings

talks

rolls

snores

plays

The radio plays.

Growing a Garden

Write two sentences that tell about the garden.

First, choose a **noun.**

Then choose an **adjective.**

Now write a sentence using both words.

Your sentence should start with the word **The.**

Writing

Describing sentences

Brain Box

Some sentences use **adjectives** to describe things.

An adjective is used in a sentence to describe something.

Example:
The ball is **blue.**

The word **blue** is an adjective. It describes the **ball.**

NOUNS

carrot

corn

cucumber

pumpkin

tomato

ADJECTIVES

big

orange

pink

red

tall

The pumpkin
is big.

Writing

Describing
sentences

Monster Mash

Write four sentences about Monster.

Use a **verb,** an **adjective,** and a **noun** for each sentence.

Start each sentence with **Monster.**

NOUNS

bugs

balls

candy

slime

ADJECTIVES

red

spooky

funny

green

VERBS

eats

throws

licks

drinks

Writing

Creative
writing

Monster eats red bugs.

At the Dog Park

Write a sentence about each dog
Use a **noun**, a **verb**, and an **adjective** in each sentence.

_____

- -

_____

_____

Writing

Creative writing

_____

- -

_____

_____

Brain Box

Remember: All sentences begin with a **capital letter** and end with a **period.**

Writing

Creative
writing

What Do You See?

Draw something you see in the box.

Writing

Creative
writing

Think of words that tell about your picture.
Write two sentences about your picture using
these words.

_____

- -

_____

- -

_____

- -

_____

- -

_____

Sequencing and Sorting

Up, Up, and Away!

Number the pictures from 1 to 4 to show what happens in order.

Welcome to the Club!

Number the pictures from 1 to 4 to show what happens in order.

Dog Wash

Number the pictures from 1 to 4 to show what happens in order.

Lunchtime!

Number the pictures from 1 to 6 to show what happens in order.

A Chick Is Born

Draw a line from each picture to the correct number on the time line to show what happens in order.

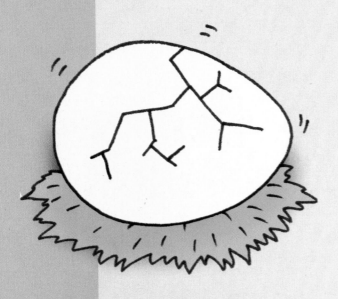

1	2	3

4   5   6

Growing Tall!

Draw a line from each picture to the correct number on the time line to show what happens in order.

1	2	3

4   5   6

Search and Sort

Look at the **numbers** in the clouds.
Write them in **numerical order** below the balloon.

Sequencing
and Sorting

Sorting

NUMBERS

Look at the **letters** in the clouds.
Write them in **alphabetical order** below the balloon.

t

p

a

z

i

LETTERS

_____

_____

_____

Sorting Shapes

Draw a line to match the things to the shapes.

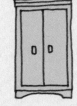

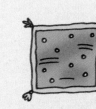

Shopping Sort

Draw a line to put each thing in the correct shopping basket below.

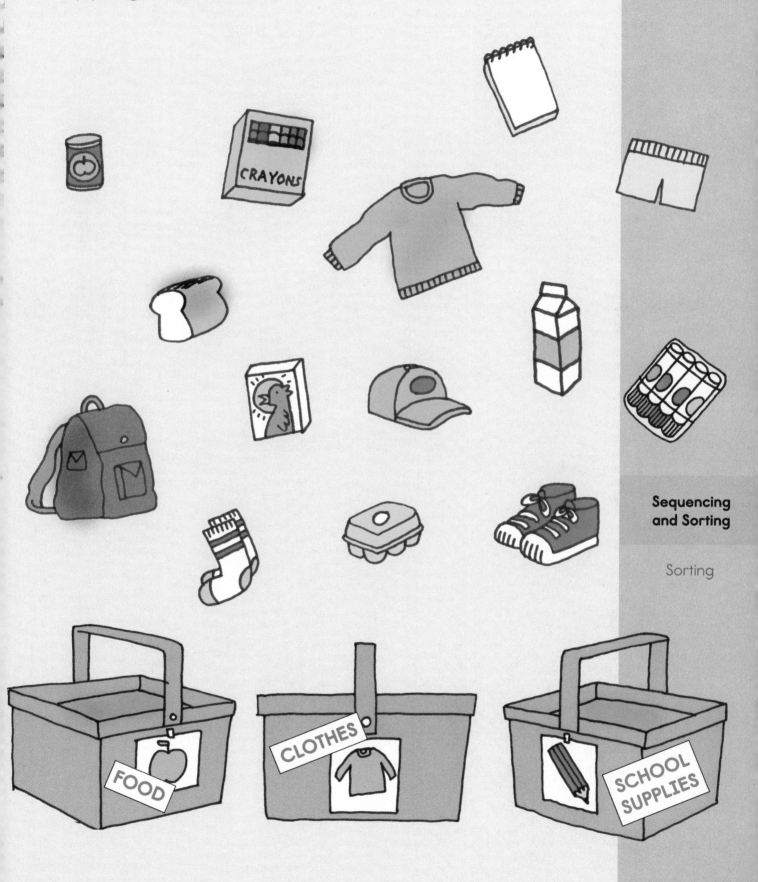

CRAYONS

FOOD

CLOTHES

SCHOOL SUPPLIES

Fun in the Snow

Look at each picture.

What happens next?

Finish the snowman for the kids.

Math Skills

Moving Day

Draw a line from the box to the matching number of things.

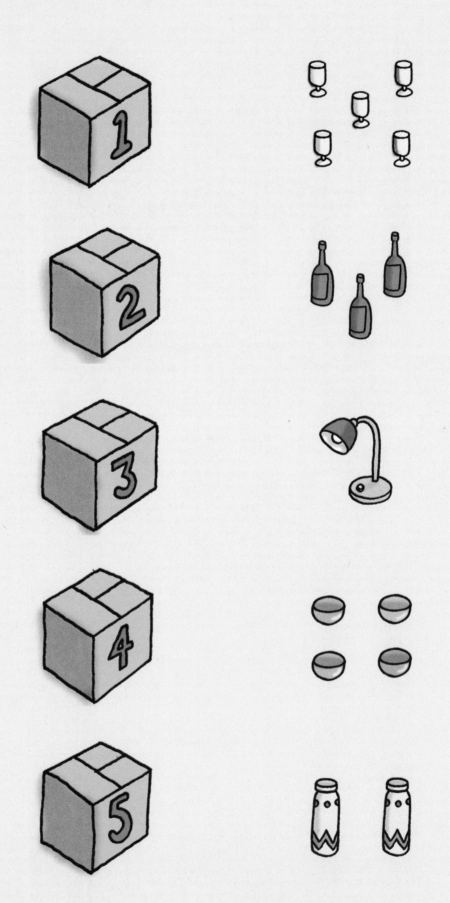

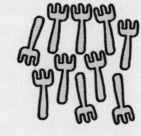

Math Skills

Number
recognition

Count Dracula!

Fill in the missing numbers.
Go across and write the
numbers in order.

1		3	4			7	8	9	
	12	13			16			19	
21	22		24			27	28		
	33	34	35	36	37				40
	42			45			48	49	
51	52	53	54				58		60
	62				66	67		69	
71		73		75		77		79	
81	82	83					88		
	92			95		97			

Counting Crayons

Write the number of crayons below each group.

_____

_____

_____

_____

_____

_____

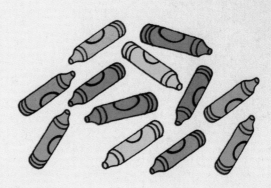

_____

_____

_____

Now say the numbers out loud.

You are counting by 2s!

Math Skills

Skip counting by 2s

Counting Fish

Write the number of fish below each group.

Say the numbers out loud.

You are counting by 2s!

_____
- - - - - - - - -
_____

_____
- - - - - - - - -

Orange Trees

Write the number of oranges below each tree.
Say the numbers out loud.
You are counting by 5s!

Math Skills

Skip counting
by 5s

At the Market

Write the number of things below each group.

_____

_____

_____

_____

Math Skills

Skip counting
by 10s

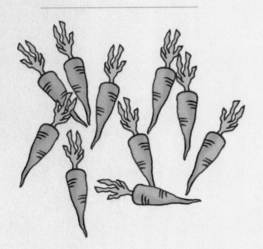

_____

_____

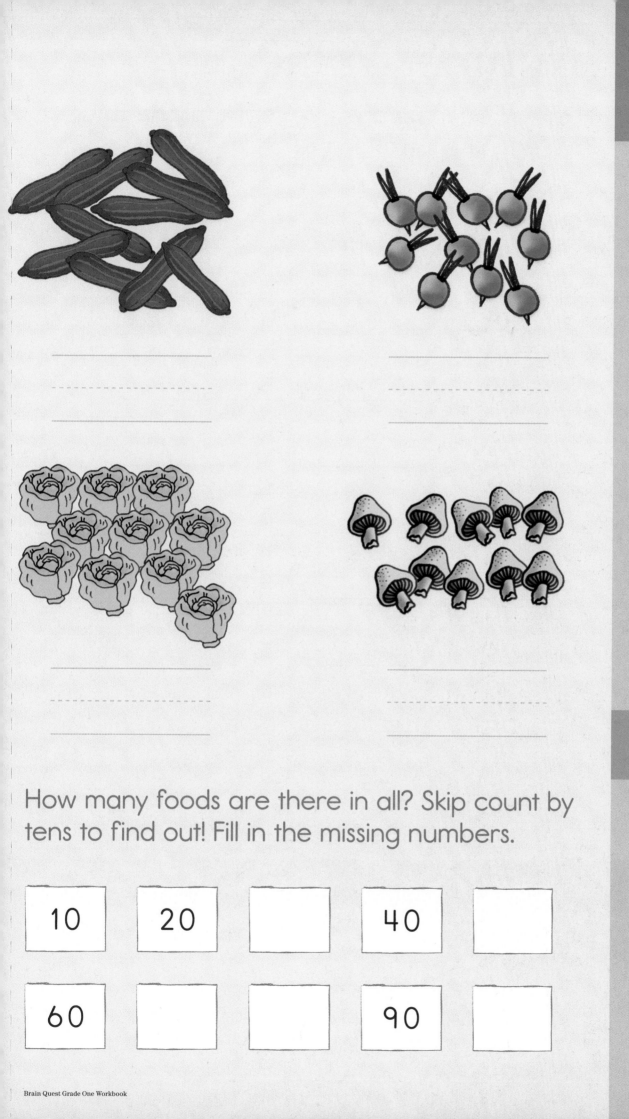

Math Skills

Skip counting
by 10s

How many foods are there in all? Skip count by tens to find out! Fill in the missing numbers.

| 10 | 20 | | 40 | |
| 60 | | | 90 | |

184

Number Value

Look at each number. Write the **place value** for each numeral on the chart.

	tens	ones
35	3	5
47	___	___
26	___	___
82	___	___
73	___	___
19	___	___
66	___	___

Math Skills

Place value to tens

Brain Box

You can use **place value** to figure out how much numerals are worth. Look at the number **25**.

tens	ones
2	5

The **5** tells us there are **5** ones. The **2** tells us there are **2** tens.

Tens and Ones

Look at each number.
Then answer the questions.

23   How many tens? __2__   ones? __3__

16   How many tens? _____   ones? _____

67   How many tens? _____   ones? _____

49   How many tens? _____   ones? _____

91   How many tens? _____   ones? _____

38   How many tens? _____   ones? _____

84   How many tens? _____   ones? _____

86

Bouncy Balls

Count the groups of balls.
Write the numbers in the boxes.
Write the number they equal in the circle.

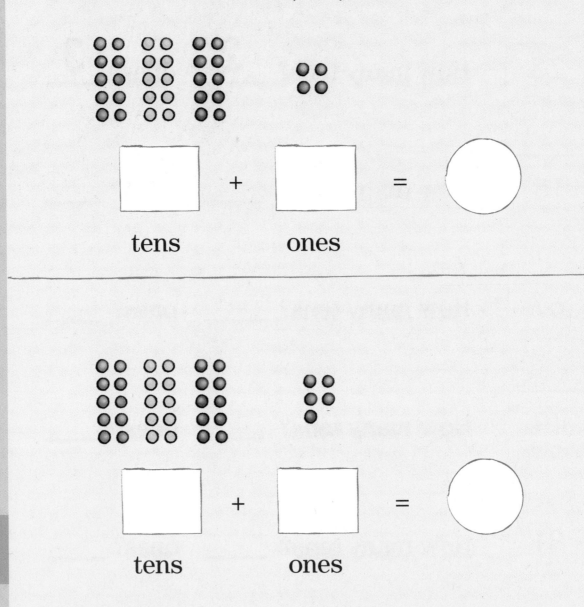

tens + ones =

tens + ones =

Math Skills**

Place value

Brain Box

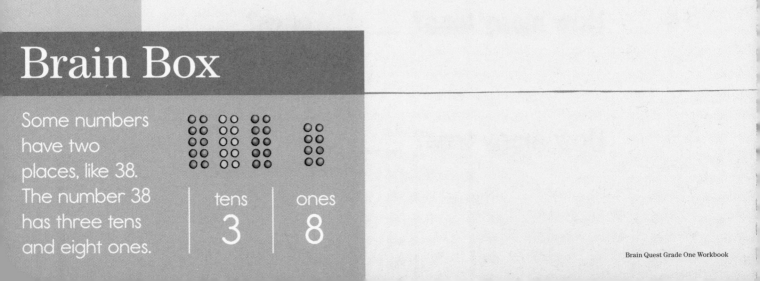

Some numbers have two places, like 38. The number 38 has three tens and eight ones.

tens	ones
3	8

ain Quest Grade One Workbook

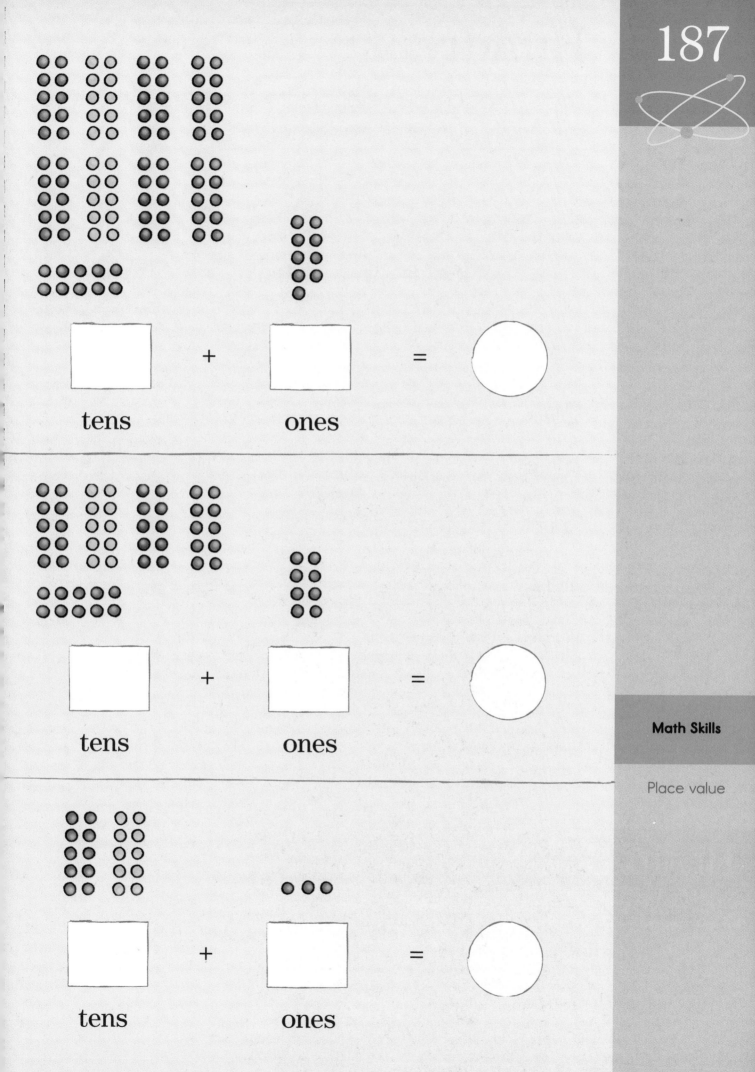

tens + ones =

tens + ones =

tens + ones =

Hundreds!

Look at each number. Write the **place value** for each numeral on the chart.

	hundreds	tens	ones
135	1	3	5
242			
528			
310			
106			
493			

Math Skills

Place value to hundreds

Brain Box

If you see three numerals, you know that the number is made up of hundreds, tens, and ones.

Look at the number **342.**

hundreds	tens	ones
3	4	2

The **3** tells us there are **3** hundreds.
The **4** tells us there are **4** tens.
The **2** tells us there are **2** ones.

You're a Star!

Count the stars on each card. Color the card that has more stars.

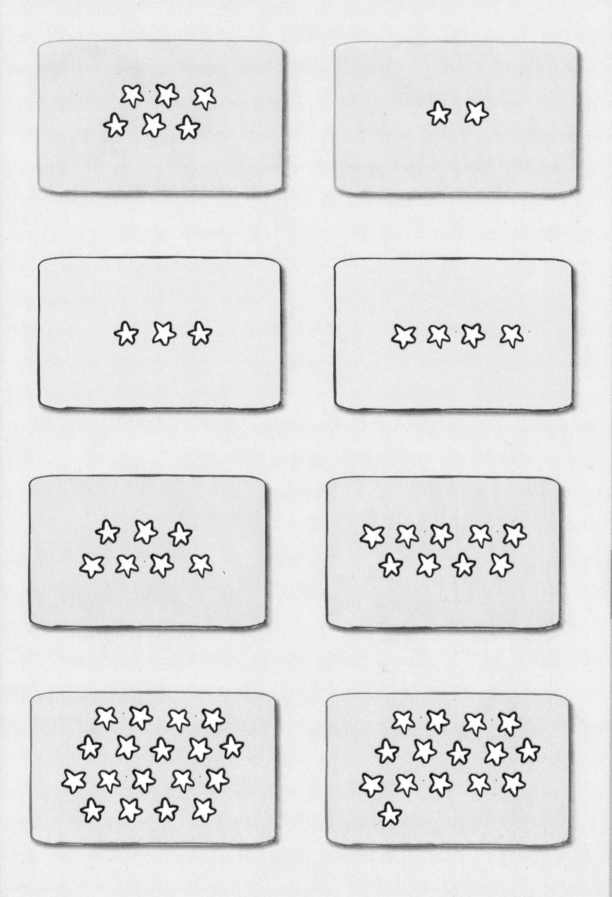

Math Skills

Greater than,
lesser than

Bake Sale

Count the brownies on each plate.
Write the number in the box.
Then write < or > to show which
plate has more brownies.

| 5 | > | 3 |

| | | |

Brain Box

< means **less than.**
> means **greater than.**

191

Math Skills

Greater than,
less than

Brain Quest Grade One Workbook

Monster Stars

Look at this **graph.**
Circle the monster with the most gold stars.

Look at this graph.
Circle the monster with the least gold stars.

Math Skills

Graphs

Brain Box

A **graph** can help you
compare numbers.

Compare the Cupcakes

Circle the baker who baked the most cupcakes.

Circle the baker who baked the least cupcakes.

Math Skills

Graphs

Draw a line between the two bakers that baked the same number of cupcakes.

Award Winners!

For each ribbon, color a block on the bar.
Circle the animal that won the most ribbons.

Book Worm

How many books do you think you see?
Don't count them. Just take a guess!

Write the number
you guessed:

Good job! You estimated!
Now count the books.
Write the number you counted:
Were you close?

Pot of Gold

How many gold coins do you think you see?
Don't count them. Just take a guess!

Write the number you guessed:

Good job! You estimated!
Now count the coins.
Write the number you counted:
Were you close?

Snow Day!

How many snowflakes do you think you see? Don't count them. Just take a guess!
Write the number you guessed:

Math Skills

Estimation

Now count the snowflakes.
Write the number you counted:

Were you close?

Addition and Subtraction

Play Ball!

Count the balls in each group.
Write the number in the box below.
Write the **sum** in the last box.

**Addition and
Subtraction**

Addition

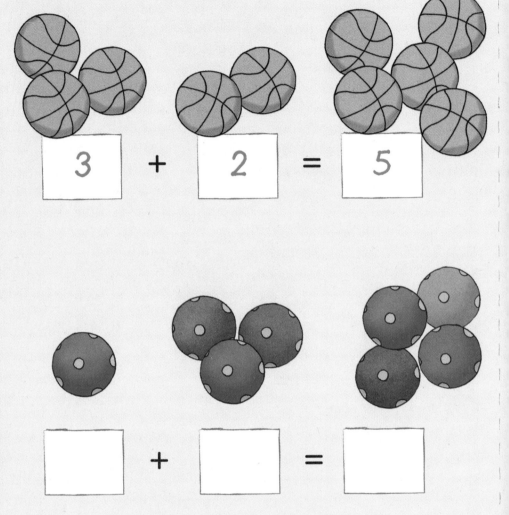

3 + 2 = 5

☐ + ☐ = ☐

Star Search

Count the stars in each group.
Write the number in the box below.
Write the **sum** in the last box.

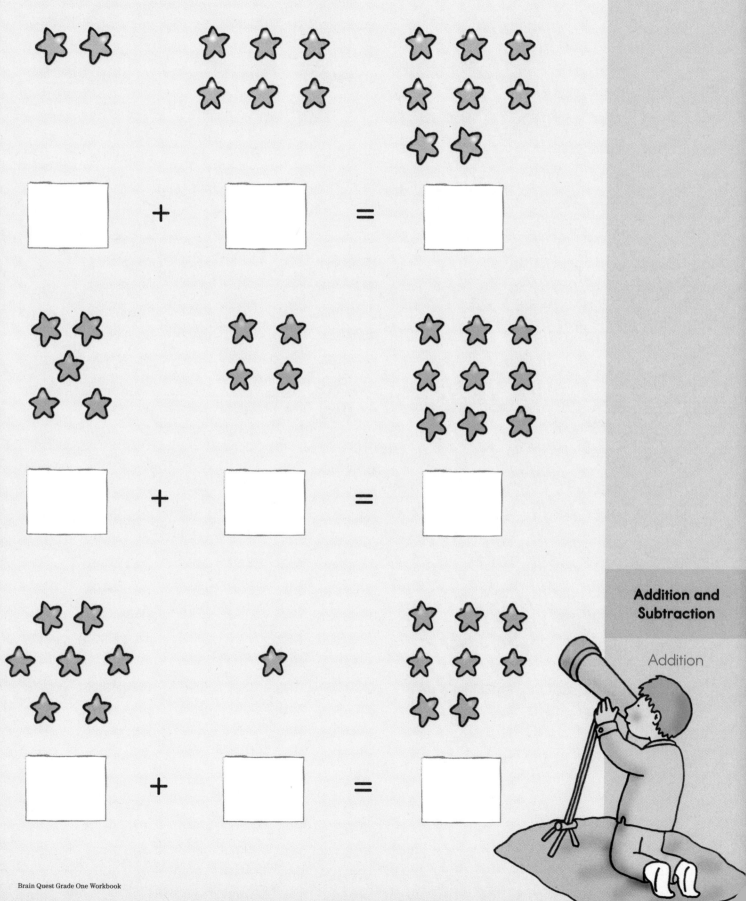

☐ + ☐ = ☐

☐ + ☐ = ☐

☐ + ☐ = ☐

At the Toy Store

Count the toys in each group.
Write the number in the box below.
Add the numbers. Write the **sum** in the last box.

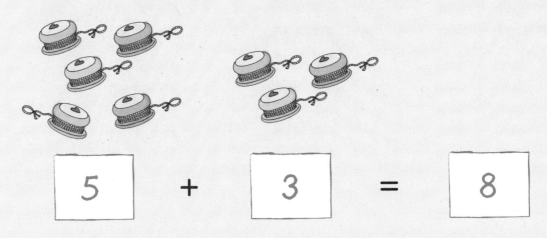

$$\boxed{5} \;+\; \boxed{3} \;=\; \boxed{8}$$

$$\boxed{} \;+\; \boxed{} \;=\; \boxed{}$$

Addition and Subtraction

Addition

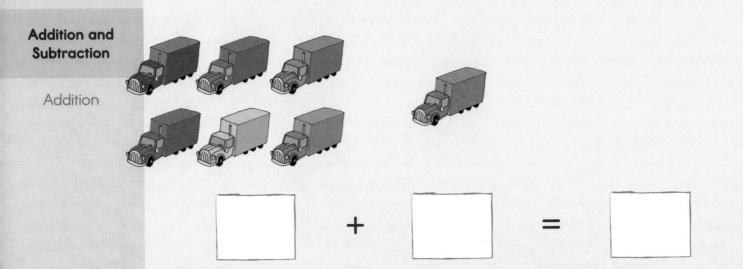

$$\boxed{} \;+\; \boxed{} \;=\; \boxed{}$$

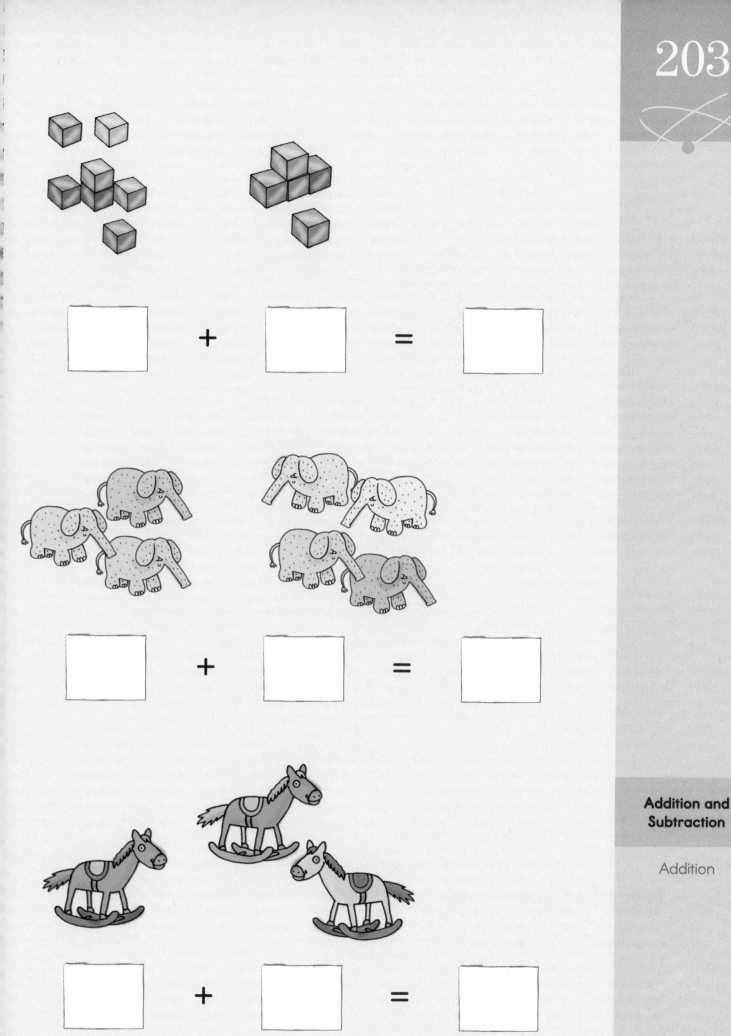

Super Scoops!

Count the scoops on each cone.

Write the number in the box.

Add the numbers to find out how many scoops there are in all.

Write the **sum** in the box below the line.

+

+

Addition and Subtraction

Addition

Brain Box

Math sentences can be written two ways:

$3 + 1 = 4$

$$\begin{array}{r} 3 \\ + 1 \\ \hline 4 \end{array}$$

Pancake Party!

Count the pancakes on each plate.

Write each number in the box.

Add the numbers to find out how many pancakes there are in all.

Write the **sum** in the box below the line.

So Many Shells!

Count the shells in each group.

Add the shells.

Draw a line to the correct answer.

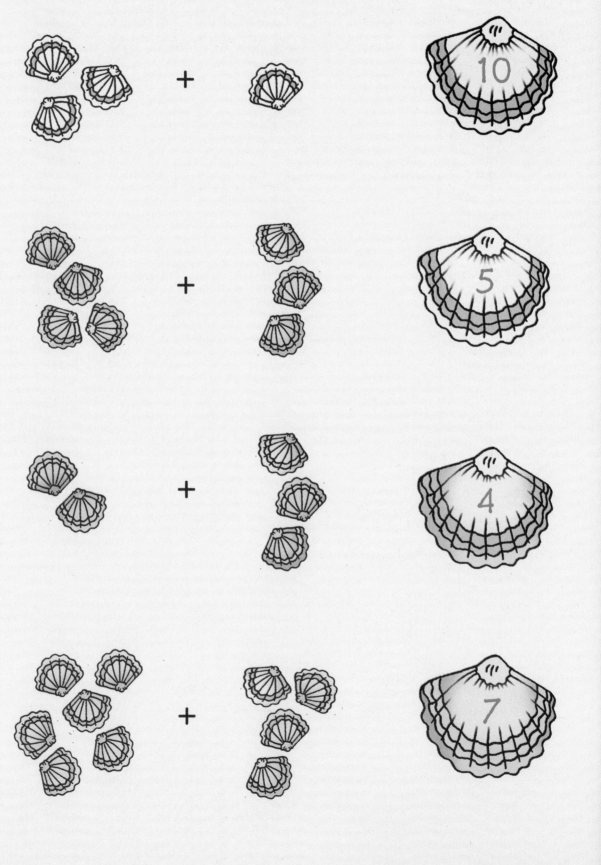

Monster Math

Add the numbers in the boxes.
Write the **sum** in the box.

3 + 5 = 8

2 + 4 =

8 + 1 =

2 + 3 =

6 + 1 =

Dragon Math

Add the numbers.

Write the **sum** in each box.

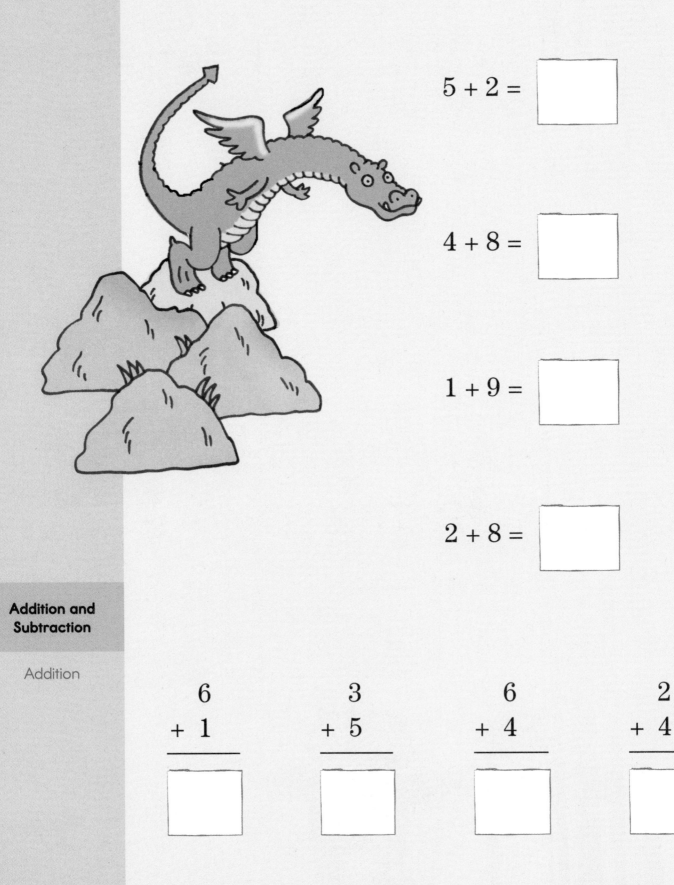

$5 + 2 =$ ☐

$4 + 8 =$ ☐

$1 + 9 =$ ☐

$2 + 8 =$ ☐

6 + 1	3 + 5	6 + 4	2 + 4
☐	☐	☐	☐

$1 + 6 =$

$7 + 5 =$

$2 + 7 =$

$4 + 8 =$

$5 + 6 =$

$7 + 6 =$

$9 + 5 =$

$10 + 3 =$

$4 + 3 =$

$5 + 5 =$

Addition and Subtraction

Addition

$$\begin{array}{r} 2 \\ + 4 \\ \hline \end{array}$$

$$\begin{array}{r} 5 \\ + 7 \\ \hline \end{array}$$

$$\begin{array}{r} 11 \\ + 4 \\ \hline \end{array}$$

$$\begin{array}{r} 4 \\ + 7 \\ \hline \end{array}$$

Bear Numbers

Add the numbers.

Write the **sum** in each box.

$6 + 4 =$ ▢

$3 + 2 =$ ▢

$7 + 7 =$ ▢

$4 + 1 =$ ▢

$2 + 6 =$ ▢

$5 + 4 =$ ▢

Addition and Subtraction

Addition

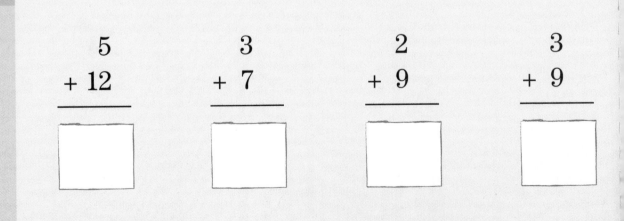

$$\begin{array}{r} 5 \\ + 12 \\ \hline \end{array}$$

$$\begin{array}{r} 3 \\ + 7 \\ \hline \end{array}$$

$$\begin{array}{r} 2 \\ + 9 \\ \hline \end{array}$$

$$\begin{array}{r} 3 \\ + 9 \\ \hline \end{array}$$

3 + 2 = ⬜

8 + 4 = ⬜

4 + 7 = ⬜

2 + 10 = ⬜

7 + 2 = ⬜

4 + 10 = ⬜

3 + 9 = ⬜

5 + 6 = ⬜

9 + 2 = ⬜

10 + 4 = ⬜

$$\begin{array}{r} 6 \\ +\ 2 \\ \hline \end{array}$$
⬜

$$\begin{array}{r} 5 \\ +\ 3 \\ \hline \end{array}$$
⬜

$$\begin{array}{r} 8 \\ +\ 1 \\ \hline \end{array}$$
⬜

$$\begin{array}{r} 1 \\ +\ 8 \\ \hline \end{array}$$
⬜

Terrific 20!

Count the insects in each group.
Write the number in the box below.
Add the numbers.
Write the **sum** in the box.

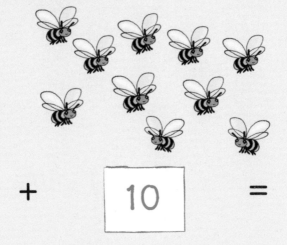

| 10 | + | 10 | = | 20 |

| | + | | = | |

Addition and Subtraction

Adding to 20

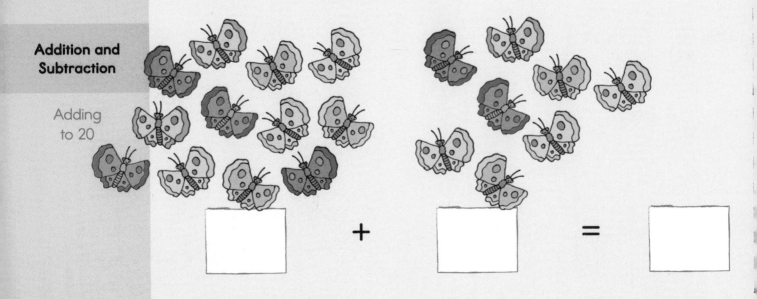

| | + | | = | |

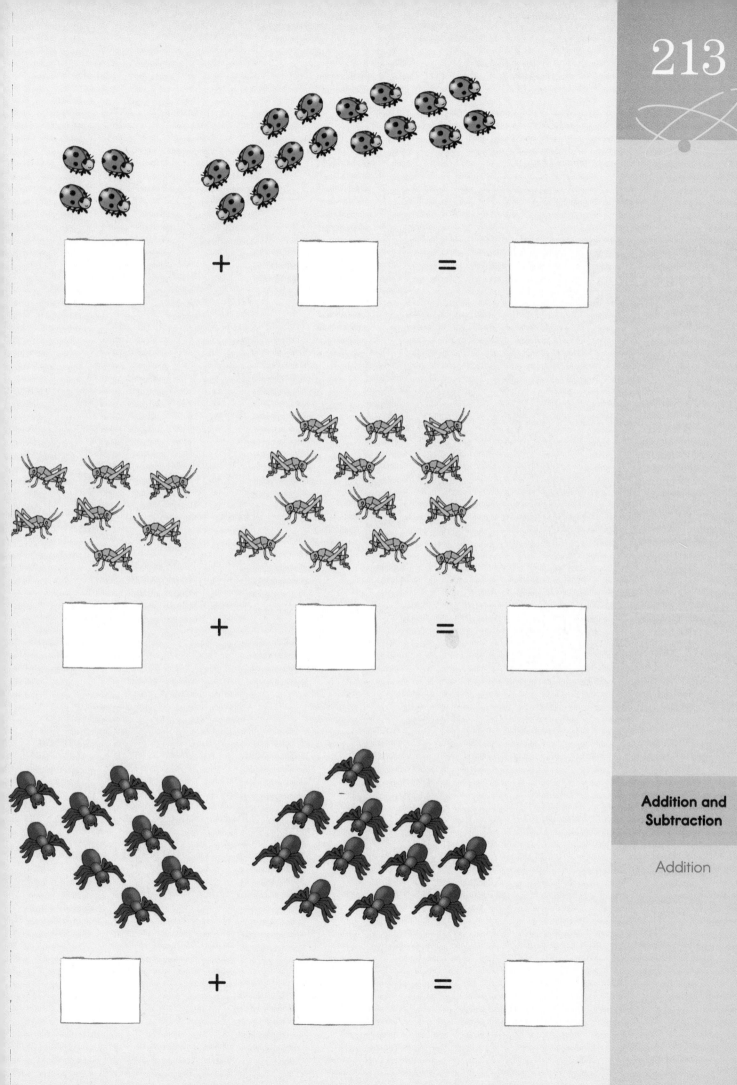

Take a Slice!

Count the slices in each pizza.
Count the number of slices taken away.
Write the number of slices that are left.

Addition and Subtraction

Subtraction

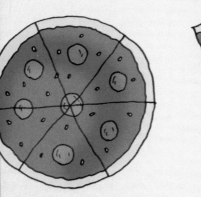  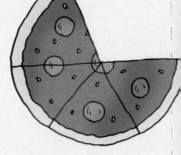

6 − 2 = 4

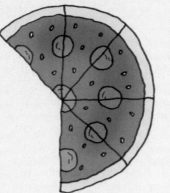 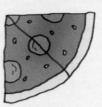 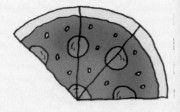

☐ − ☐ = ☐

Balloon Pop

Count the balloons.
Count the balloons that have flown away.
Write how many are left.

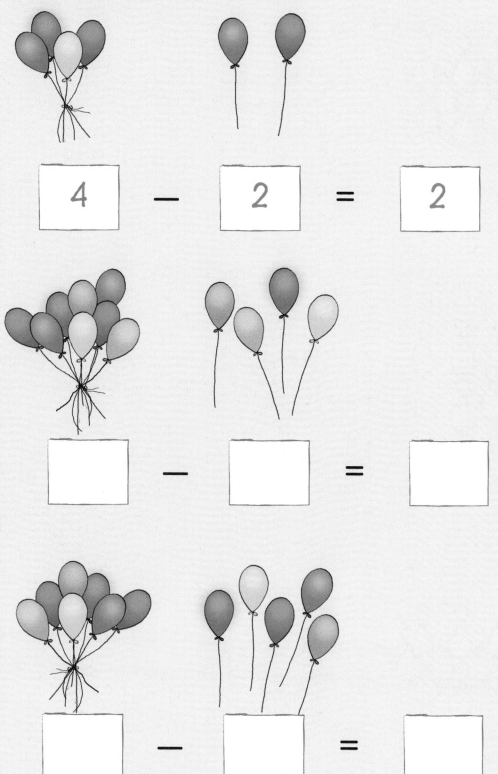

| 4 | − | 2 | = | 2 |

| | − | | = | |

| | − | | = | |

Let's Bowl!

Count how many pins are standing.
Count how many pins fall.
Subtract to tell how many pins are left.

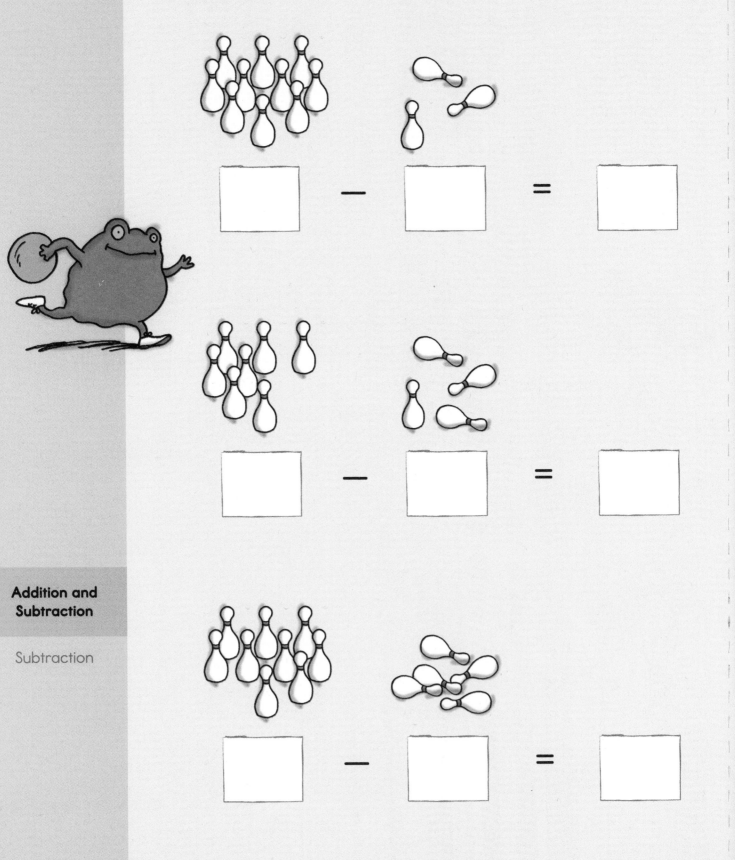

$$\boxed{} - \boxed{} = \boxed{}$$

$$\boxed{} - \boxed{} = \boxed{}$$

$$\boxed{} - \boxed{} = \boxed{}$$

**Addition and
Subtraction**

Subtraction

Doggy Dessert

Count the dog bones.

Count how many bones the dog eats.

Subtract to tell how many bones are left.

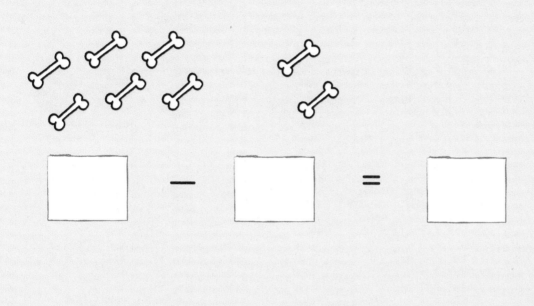

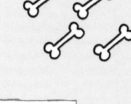

[ ] − [ ] = [ ]

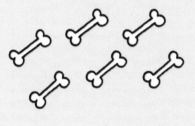

[ ] − [ ] = [ ]

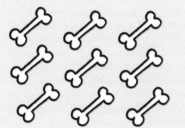

[ ] − [ ] = [ ]

Falling Leaves

Count the leaves.
Count how many leaves fly away.
Subtract to tell how many are left.

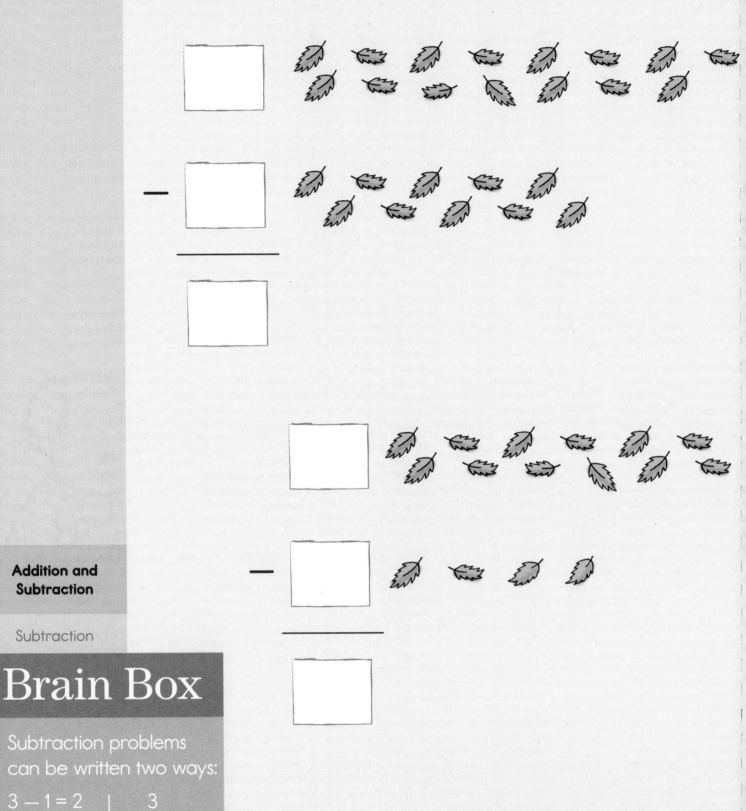

Brain Box

Subtraction problems
can be written two ways:

$3 - 1 = 2$

$$\begin{array}{r} 3 \\ -1 \\ \hline 2 \end{array}$$

Shooting Stars

Count the stars in the sky.

Count how many stars shoot away.

Subtract to tell how many stars are left.

Write the numbers on the lines.

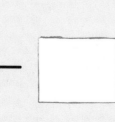

Brain Quest Grade One Workbook

Go in the Snow!

Subtract the numbers.
Write the **difference** in the box.

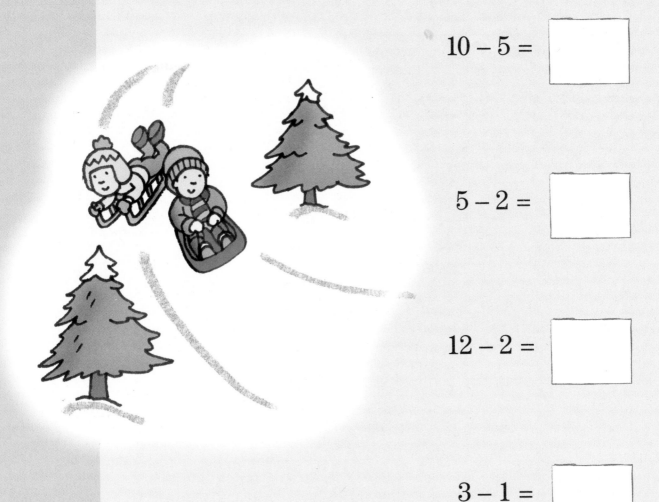

$10 - 5 =$ ☐

$5 - 2 =$ ☐

$12 - 2 =$ ☐

$3 - 1 =$ ☐

Addition and Subtraction

Subtraction

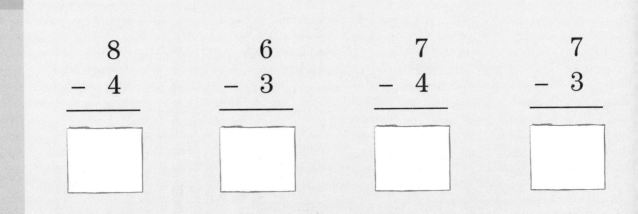

$$\begin{array}{r} 8 \\ -\ 4 \\ \hline \end{array}$$
☐

$$\begin{array}{r} 6 \\ -\ 3 \\ \hline \end{array}$$
☐

$$\begin{array}{r} 7 \\ -\ 4 \\ \hline \end{array}$$
☐

$$\begin{array}{r} 7 \\ -\ 3 \\ \hline \end{array}$$
☐

7 − 1 =

5 − 2 =

5 − 3 =

10 − 3 =

9 − 5 =

7 − 6 =

8 − 2 =

9 − 8 =

4 − 2 =

4 − 3 =

$$\begin{array}{r} 2 \\ -\ 1 \\ \hline \end{array}$$

$$\begin{array}{r} 4 \\ -\ 4 \\ \hline \end{array}$$

$$\begin{array}{r} 8 \\ -\ 4 \\ \hline \end{array}$$

$$\begin{array}{r} 10 \\ -\ 5 \\ \hline \end{array}$$

The Magic Word

Add or **subtract** the numbers.
Write the answers in the boxes.

7 + 13 = ☐ O

10 − 5 = ☐ E

8 − 7 = ☐ P

12 − 8 = ☐ R

```
    6
+   4
```
☐ S

```
   20
−   5
```
☐ T

Figure out the wizard's magic word. Write the
letters that match the numbers in the boxes.

1	4	5	10	15	20
☐	☐	☐	☐	☐	☐

Shapes and Measurement

Balloon Blowup!

Look at the shapes of the balloons.

Color the rectangles yellow.

Color the diamonds purple.

Color the ovals pink.

Color the circles red.

Color the squares blue.

Color the triangles green.

Shapes and
Measurement

Identifying
shapes

Tell My Fortune!

Color the triangle purple.

Color the rectangle **brown**.

Color the circle gray.

Color the diamond green.

Color the ovals blue.

Quiz Me!

Answer the questions about shapes.

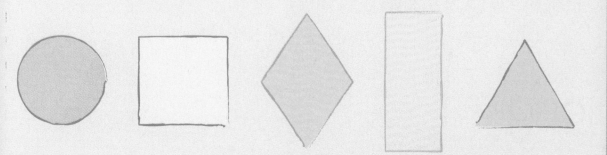

How many sides does a square have?

How many corners does a diamond have?

How many sides does a triangle have?

How many corners does a circle have?

How many corners does a rectangle have?

Shape Match

Draw a line from each card to the matching shape.

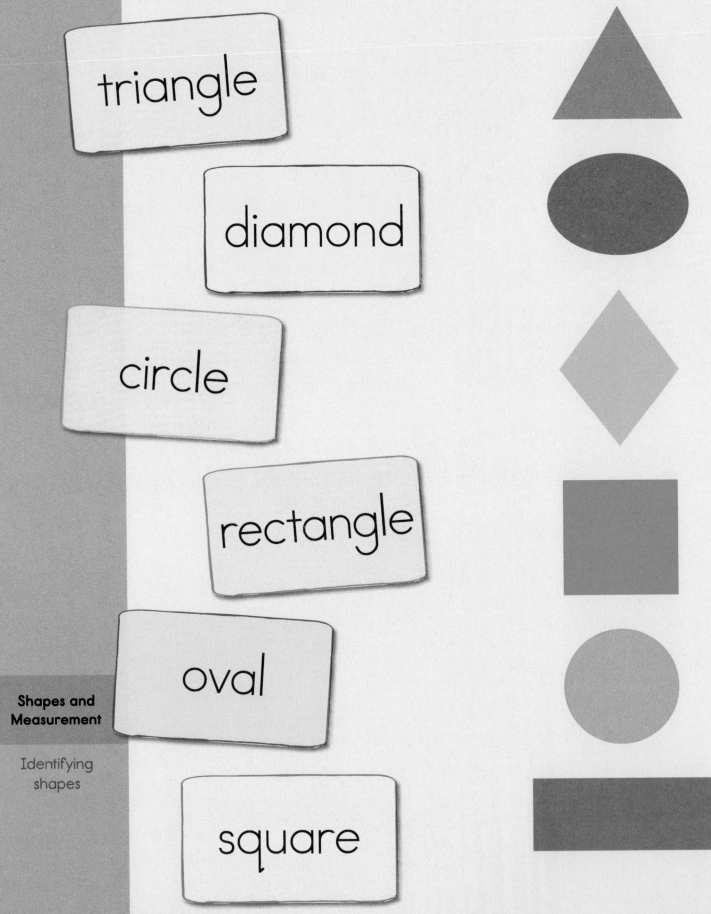

triangle

diamond

circle

rectangle

oval

square

Connect the Dots!

Connect the dots to make each shape. Color each shape the same color as the dots.

Rulers Rule!

Look at the **ruler.** It is 6 inches long.

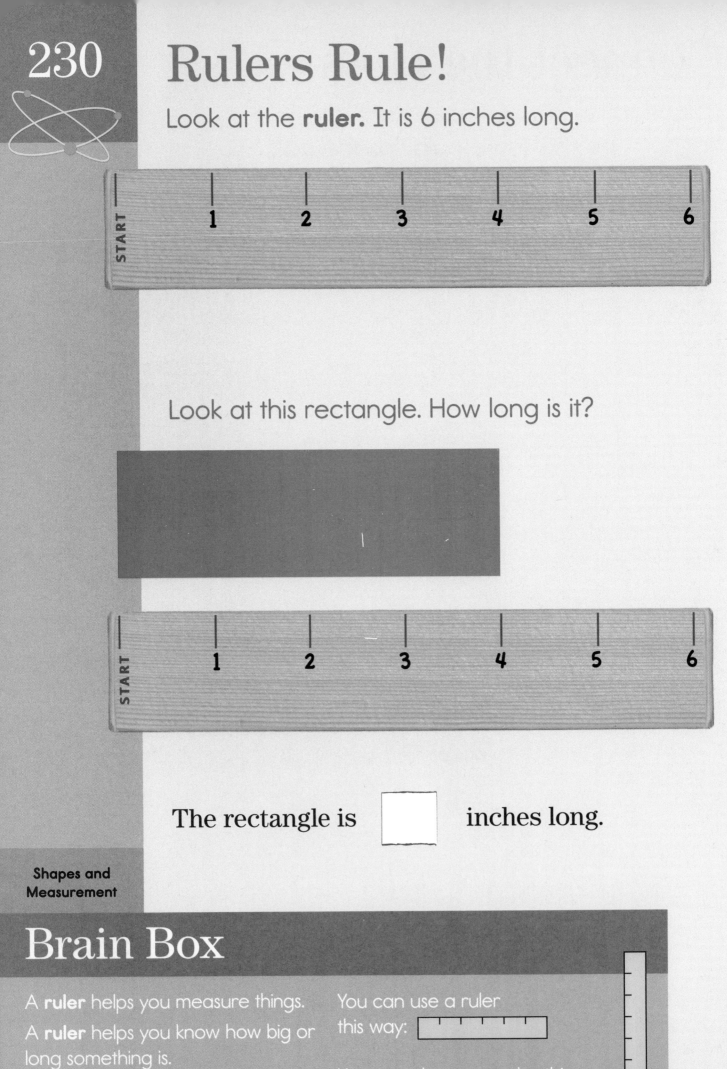

Look at this rectangle. How long is it?

The rectangle is ⬜ inches long.

Shapes and Measurement

Brain Box

A **ruler** helps you measure things.

A **ruler** helps you know how big or long something is.

Each number is an **inch.**

You can use a ruler this way:

You can also use a ruler this way:

More Rulers!

How tall is this green rectangle?

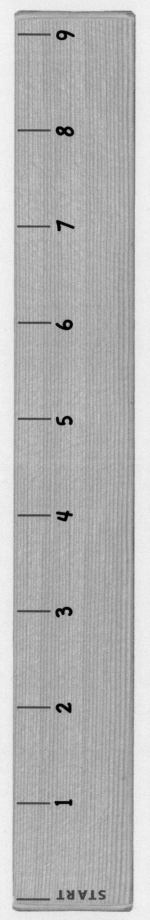

The rectangle is [ ] inches tall.

Measure the Triangle!

The sides of this purple triangle are all the same.

How long is each side?

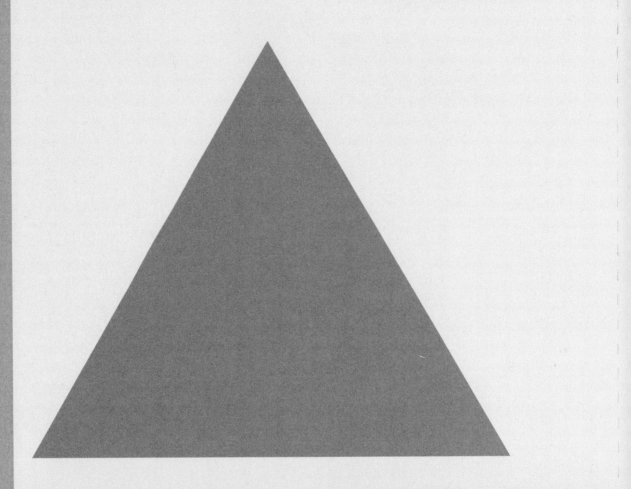

START   1   2   3   4   5   6

Each side of the triangle is ☐ inches long.

Comparing Shapes!

Measuring can help you compare.
Circle the shape that is taller.

How tall is the blue square? 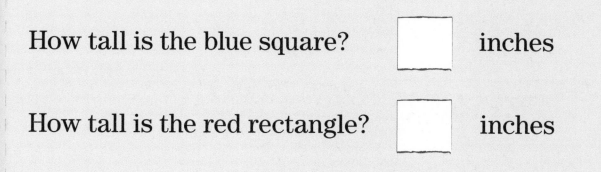 inches

How tall is the red rectangle? inches

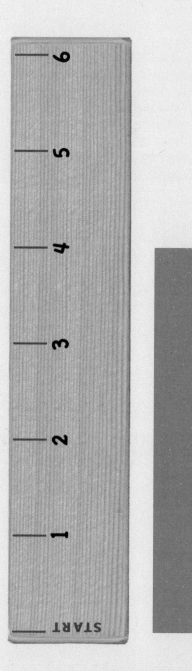

Sssssssnakes!

How long is each snake?

Write the number of inches next to each snake's head.

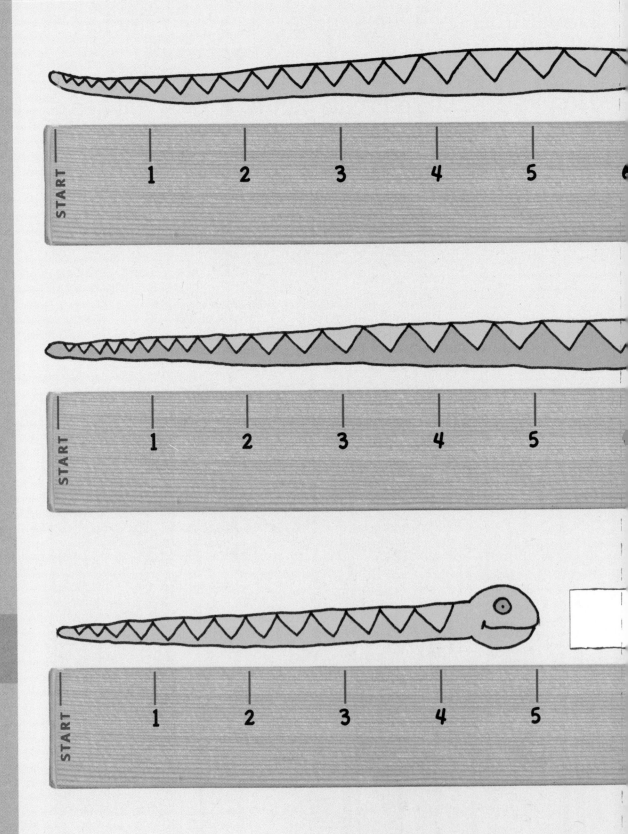

Which snake is the shortest?

Draw a circle around the shortest snake.

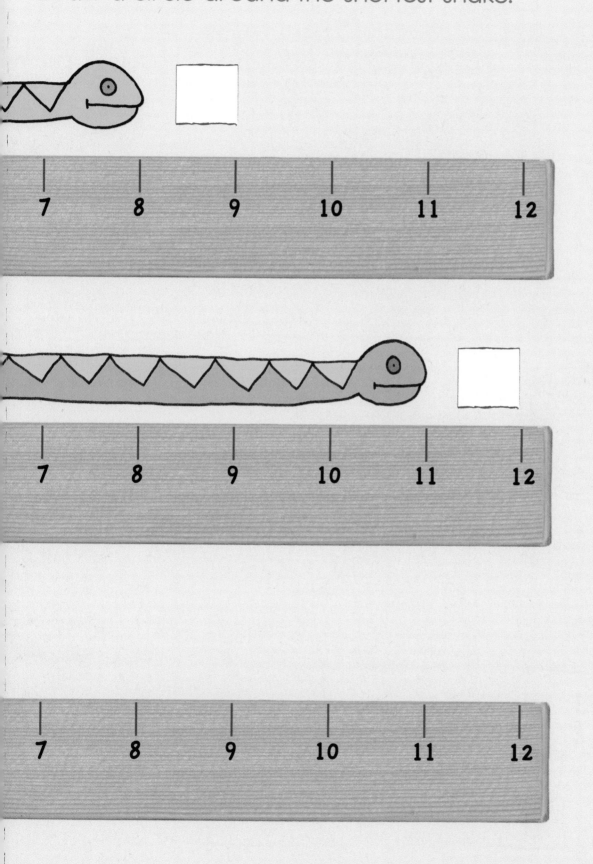

Monsters Measure!

How tall is each monster?
Write the number of inches above each monster.

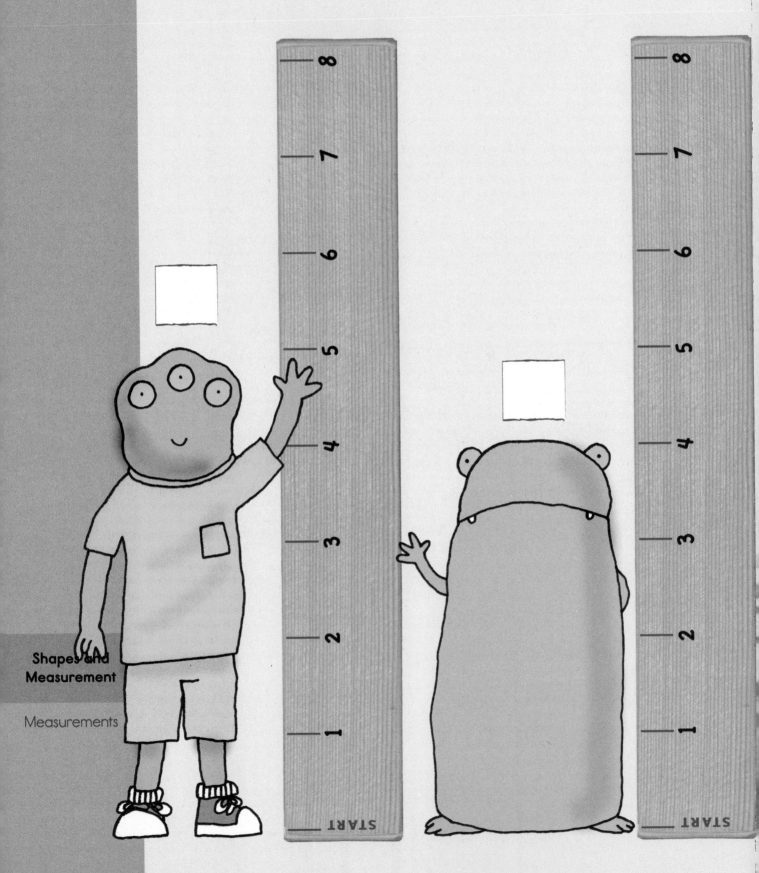

Which monster is tallest?
Circle the tallest monster.

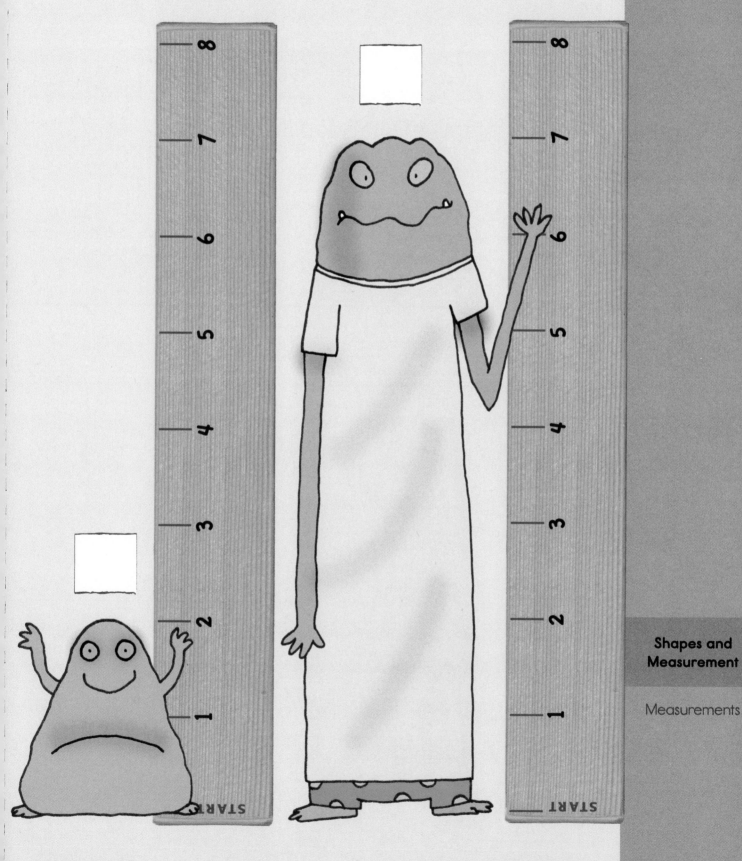

Shapes and Measurement

Measurements

Lawn Bowling

How far did each kid roll the ball?
Write the number of inches next to each ball.

1   2   3   4   5   6

1   2   3   4   5   6

1   2   3   4   5   6

Whose ball rolled the farthest?
Circle the ball that rolled the farthest.

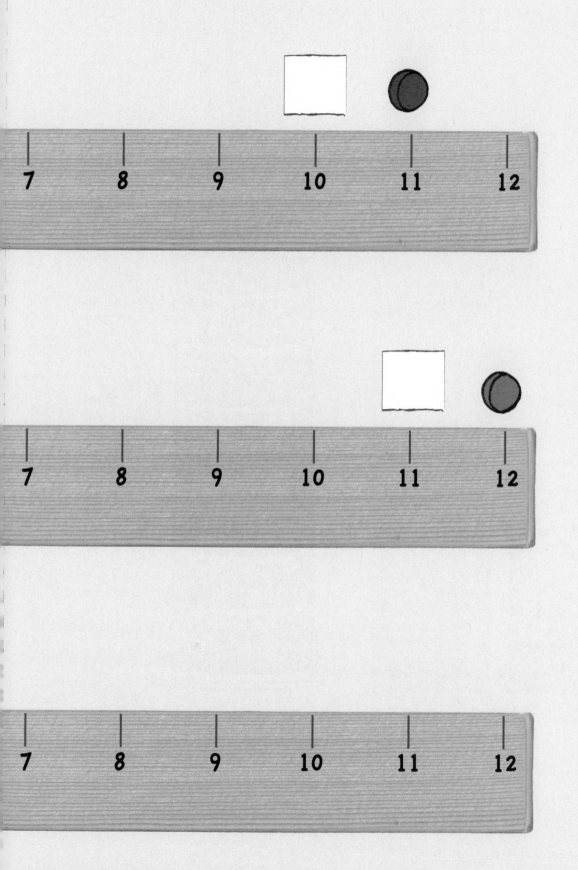

The Great Cake Bake-Off

How tall is each cake?

Write the number of inches above each cake.

Whose cake is tallest?

Draw a star beside the baker.

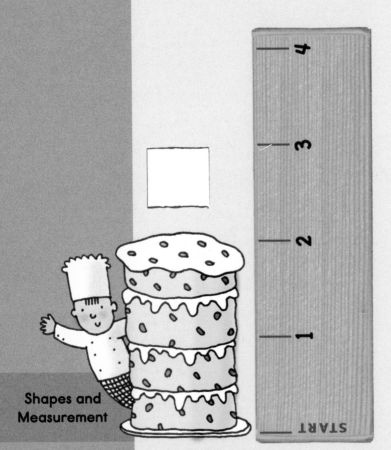

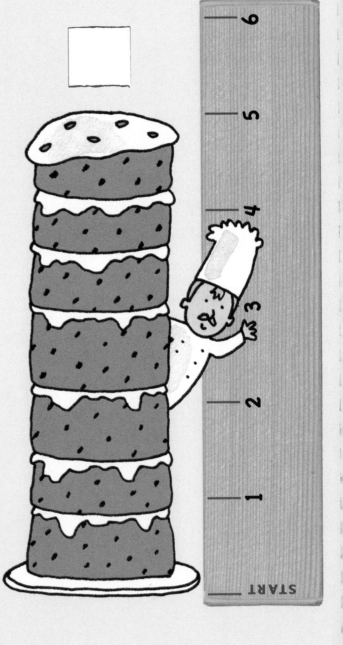

Shapes and Measurement

Measurements

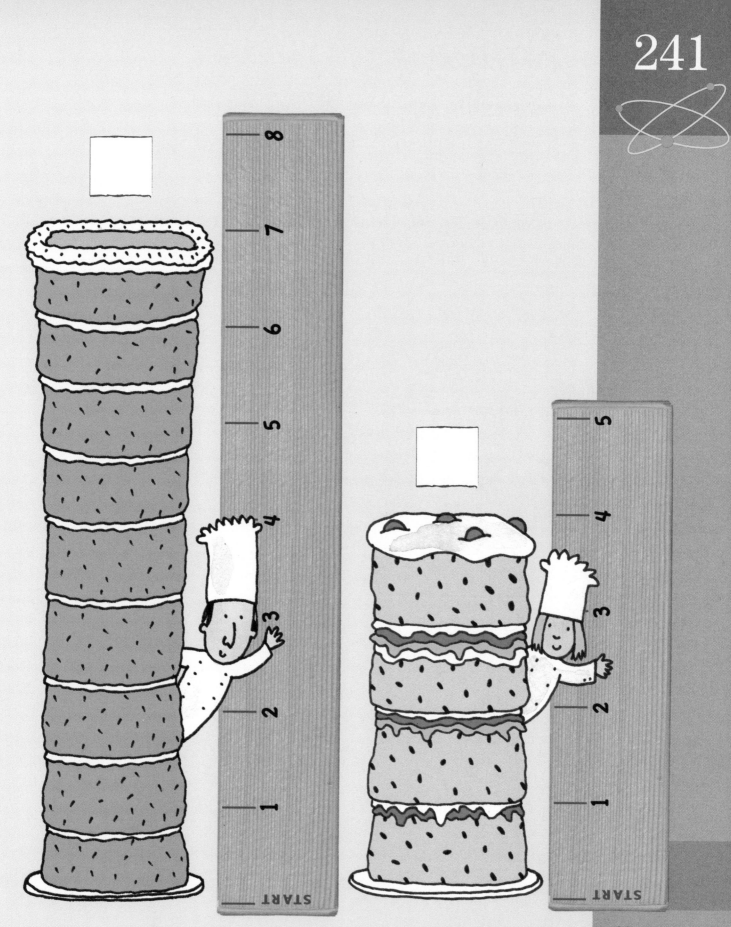

Shape Pictures

Look at the shapes.

Think of a picture you can draw with these shapes.

Draw your picture in the frame.

You can add other shapes, too.

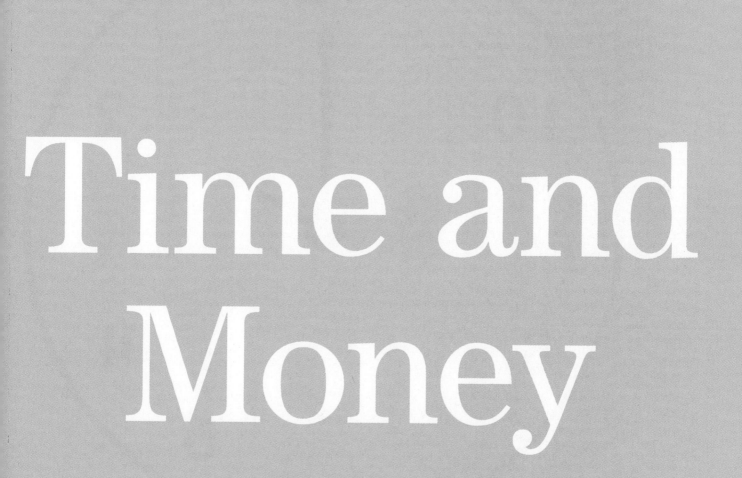

Time and Money

Broken Clock!

Can you help fix the **clock?**
Write the missing numbers in the circles.

Brain Box

A **clock** has 12 numbers. Each number stands for one hour.

A clock has a **little hand.** It points to the hour. A clock has a **big hand.** It points to the minutes.

Clock Shop

What time is it?

Write the time on the line below each clock.

3:00

_____

_____   _____

_____   _____

Time and Money

Telling time on the hour

Catch the Train!

Read the times on the train schedule.
Draw a line to the watch with that time.

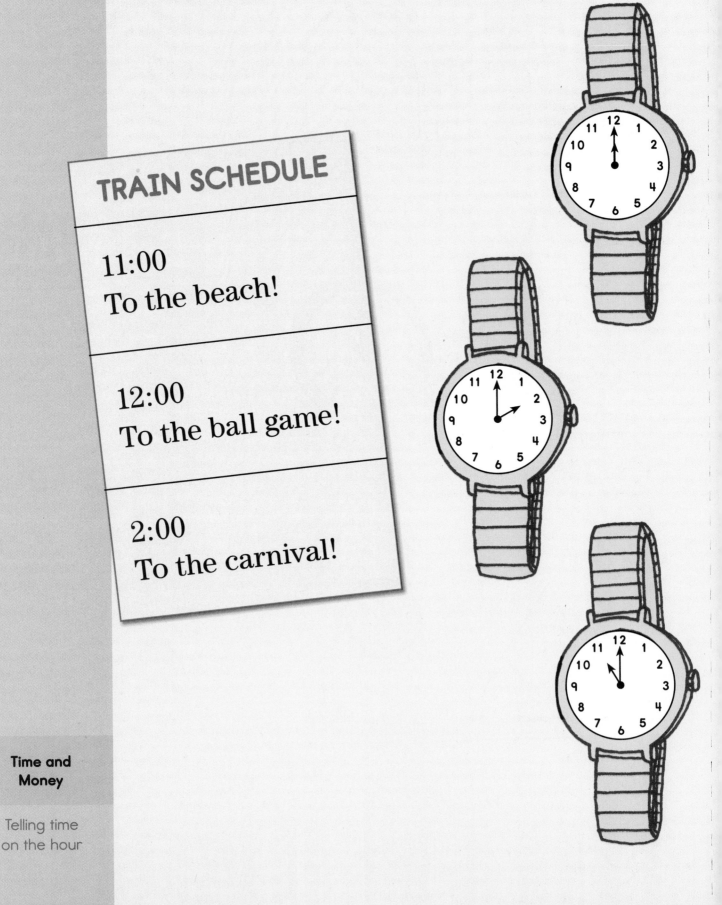

TRAIN SCHEDULE

11:00
To the beach!

12:00
To the ball game!

2:00
To the carnival!

TRAIN SCHEDULE

3:00
To the horse show!

4:00
To the pizza party!

7:00
To the mountains!

Beach   11·00
Basketball   12·00
Carnival   2·00
Horse show   3·00
Pizza Party   4·00
Mountains   7·00

Show the Half Hour

Write the time below each clock.

12:30

Brain Box

Look at this clock:

The little hand is pointing between the **3** and the **4**. The big hand is pointing to the **6**. When the big hand points to the **6**, it shows the half hour. This clock says that it is **3:30**.

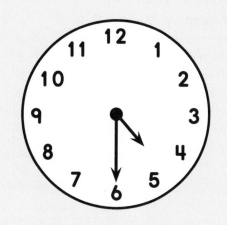

Time and Money

Telling time on the half hour

Two Kinds of Clocks

Draw a line to match the clocks that show the same time.

Time and Money

Matching clocks

Ticktock!

Draw the hands on the clock to show the time written below.

1:30

7:30

9:30

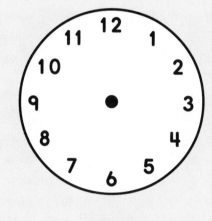

3:00

6:00

12:30

Time and Money

Telling time

Pennies, Nickels, Dimes

How many pennies make a nickel?
Count the pennies. Write the number.

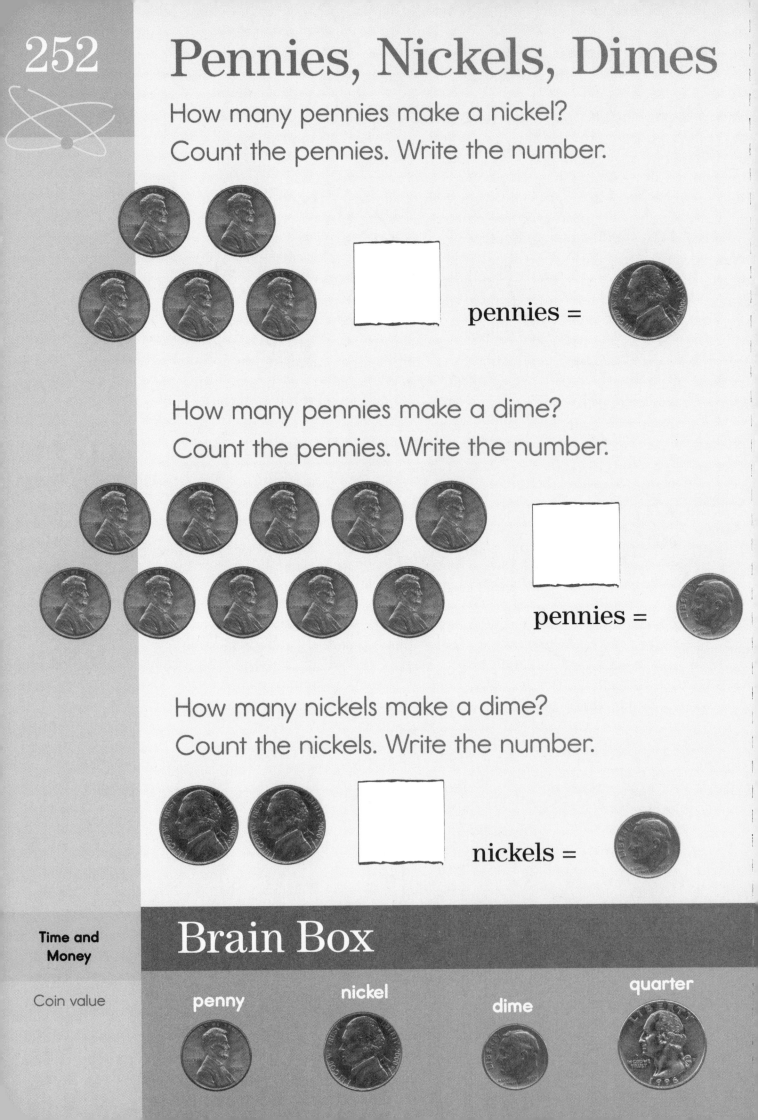

pennies =

How many pennies make a dime?
Count the pennies. Write the number.

pennies =

How many nickels make a dime?
Count the nickels. Write the number.

nickels =

Brain Box

penny   nickel   dime   quarter

Time and
Money

Coin value

Total Cents

Write the number of ¢ in the box below each coin. The symbol ¢ means cents.
Then add the money.

[ ] ¢ + [ ] ¢ = [ ] ¢

[ ] ¢ + [ ] ¢ = [ ] ¢

[ ] ¢ + [ ] ¢ = [ ] ¢

Time and Money

Counting money

Quarters

How many pennies make a quarter?
Count the pennies. Write the number.

pennies =

How else can you make a quarter?
Add the coins to find out!

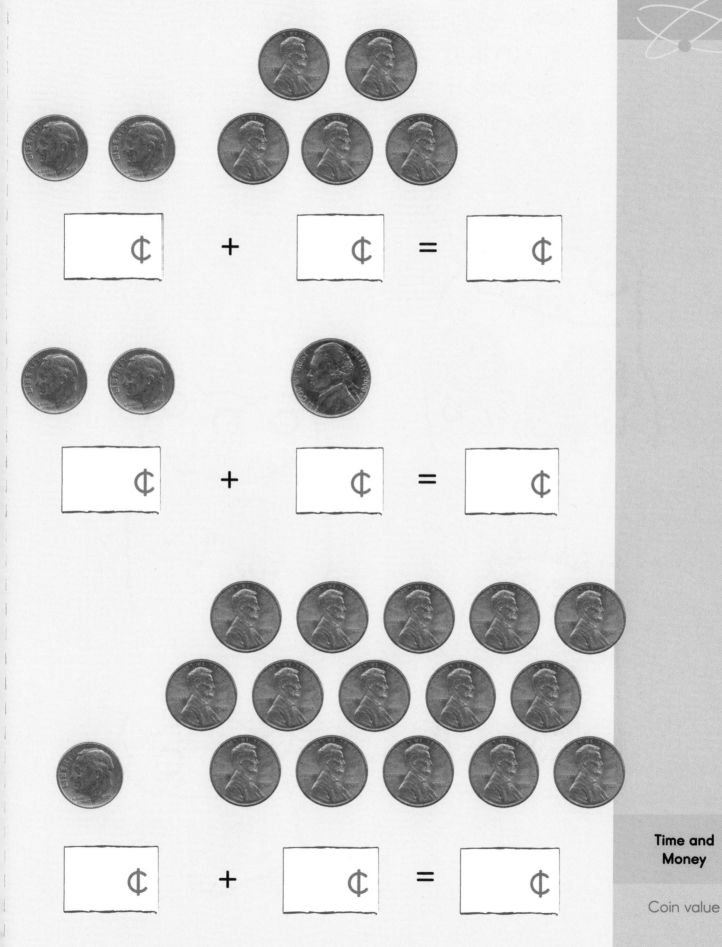

[   ] ¢ + [   ] ¢ = [   ] ¢

[   ] ¢ + [   ] ¢ = [   ] ¢

[   ] ¢ + [   ] ¢ = [   ] ¢

Lucky Monsters!

Color the monster who found the most money green.

Color the monster who found the least money red.

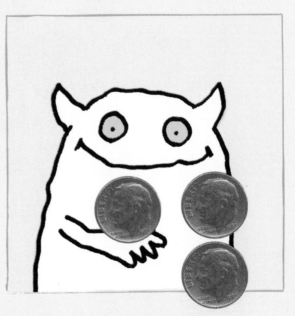

Time and Money

Identifying money

Which Is More?

Write the money value.

Circle the money that is worth the most.

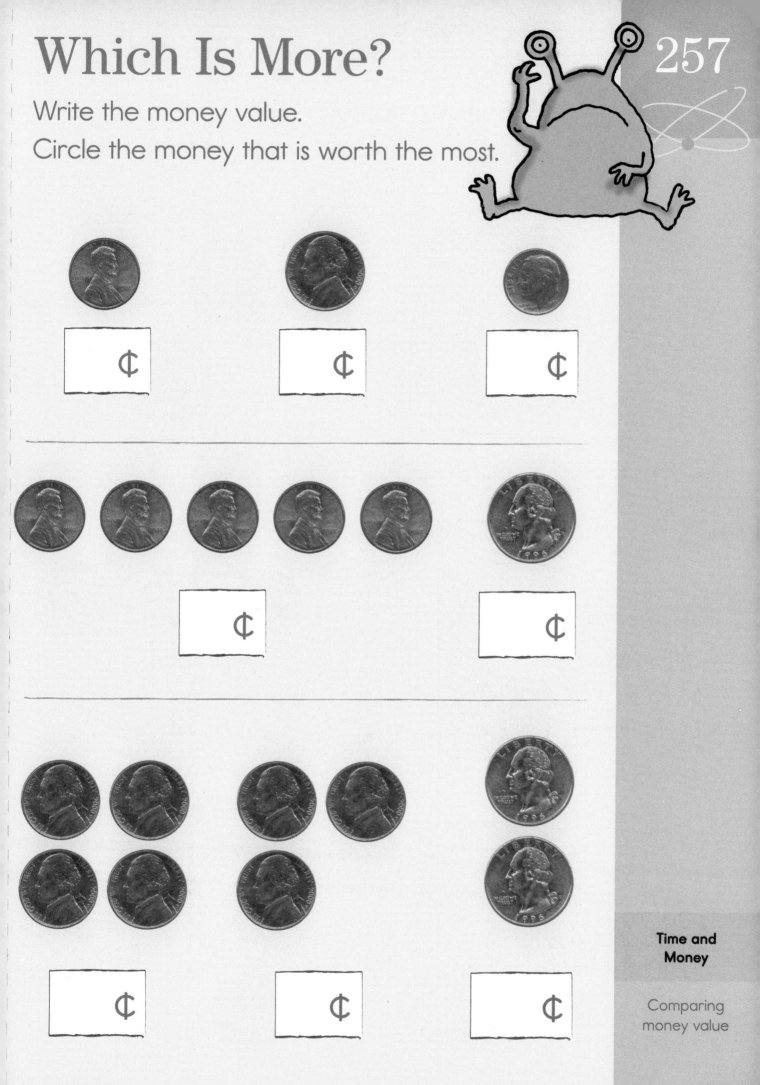

¢   ¢   ¢

¢   ¢

¢   ¢   ¢

Time and
Money

Comparing
money value

Pick the Right Price

Read the price on each vase.

Draw a line to the money you need to buy it.

Ball-game Treats

Read the price for each ball-game treat.
Draw a line to the money you need to buy it.

1 ¢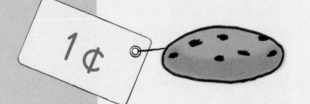

50 ¢

5 ¢

25 ¢

10 ¢

Time and Money

Money value

Social Studies

Where You Live

Complete the sentences to tell about where you live.

The name of my street is

_____

- -

_____

The name of my city or town is

_____

- -

_____

The name of my state is

_____

- -

_____

Make a Difference!

Think about your community.
Draw your favorite place.

Write a sentence about why you like this place.

Social Studies

Community
awareness

We Need Farms!

Most foods we eat and things we drink come from farms.

Circle the things we get from farms.

Social Studies

Goods and
services

Got Milk?

Milk comes from cows!

It starts at a farm and ends up at a store.

Number the pictures from 1 to 6 to show how it gets there.

1

From the Farm

The plants on the left were grown on farms. Draw a line to match each plant to the food we get from it.

Things to Buy

People make the things we buy.
Draw a line to match the person with
the thing he or she made.

Travel by Truck

Trucks take the things people make to the store.

Help this truck get to the store.
Draw a line down the correct road.

Street Maps

Draw a red line down the streets to get the kids to school.
Try to find the shortest way.

Draw a **blue** line down the streets to get the kids to the museum.
Try to find the shortest way.

Day at the Fair

Draw a red line down the path to
the Ferris wheel.

Draw a blue line down to
the fun house.

GAMES

FAIR

Draw a green line down to the games.
Draw an orange line down to the hot dog stand.

It's a Sign!

The letters on these signs are all mixed up! Unscramble the letters on each sign and write the correct word below.

_____

_____

_____

_____

Science

Our Earth

Read about the Earth. On the globe below, color all the land parts brown. Color all the water parts blue.

Earth is the planet we live on.

It has land and water.

land

water

land

water

land

The Sun

Read about the sun.

Write the answers to the questions on the lines below.

The sun is a star.

The sun is very important.

It gives us light.

It gives us heat.

Without the sun, we could not survive.

The Earth travels around the sun once per year.

This is called an orbit.

Is the sun a moon or a star?

_____

_____

What does the sun give us?

_____

_____

Sun

Science

Night and Day

Read about night and day. Write the answers to the questions on the lines below.

Earth spins as it orbits around the sun.

When Earth is facing the sun, it is day.

The sun shines on Earth during the day, so it is light.

When Earth is facing away from the sun, it is night.

The sun doesn't shine on Earth at night, so it is dark.

What does Earth do as it orbits around the sun?

....

When Earth faces the sun, is it day or night?

....

The Seasons

Look at each picture.

Write the season name below the picture.

Use the words from the Word Box.

| winter | spring | summer | fall |

Lots of Weather

Look at each picture.
Describe the weather in each picture using a word from the Word Box.

| sunny | rainy | snowy | windy |

What's the Weather?

Keep a weather log for one week.
Then write an adjective to tell about
the weather for each day.

Monday

Tuesday

Wednesday

Thursday

Friday

Saturday

Sunday

Plants and the Sun

Find the plants in the picture.
Color them green.

Plant Life Cycles

Number the pictures from 1 to 6
to show the life cycle of an apple tree.

All living things
follow a life cycle.

They are born.

They grow.

They reproduce.

They die.

Life cycles

Butterfly Life Cycle

Read about the butterfly's life cycle. Then label each stage of the life cycle on the picture.

A butterfly is an insect. All insects follow a life cycle.

First, a butterfly lays an egg.

The egg hatches into a caterpillar.

After eating a lot, the caterpillar spins a chrysalis.

Inside the chrysalis, the caterpillar turns into an adult.

Soon, the adult emerges, or comes out, from the chrysalis.

A new butterfly is born!

Life cycles

A Person's Life Cycle

Draw yourself as a baby.

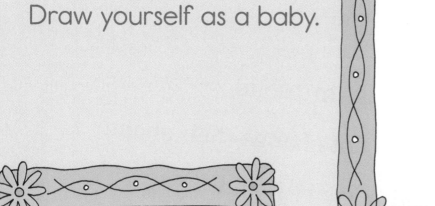

Draw yourself now.

Draw yourself as a grown-up!

Life cycles

Solids and Liquids

Read about solids and liquids.
Write the letter **S** below the solid things.
Write the letter **L** below the liquid things.

> Some things are solid.
>
> Solids do not change their shape.
>
> Some things are liquid.
>
> Liquids can change shape.

It's Good to Recycle!

Read about recycling.
Circle the things at this party that can be recycled.

We can turn old things into new things.

This is called recycling.

We can recycle cans.

We can recycle paper.

We can recycle bottles.

Drop It in the Bin

Look at the picture on each bin.

Draw a line from all the things you can recycle
to the correct bin.

Answer Key

(For pages not included in this section, answers will vary.)

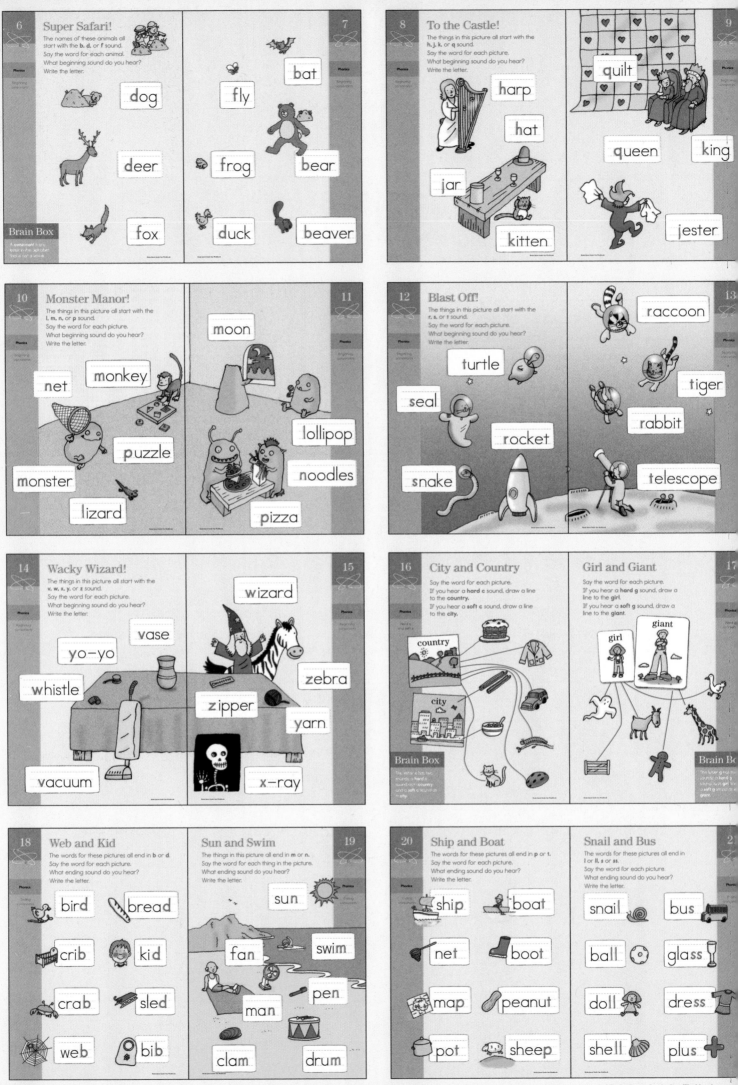

Super Safari!

6

The names of these animals all start with the **b**, **d**, or **f** sound.
Say the word for each animal.
What beginning sound do you hear?
Write the letter.

dog

deer

fox

Brain Box

7

fly

bat

frog

bear

duck

beaver

To the Castle!

8

The things in this picture all start with the **h**, **j**, **k**, or **q** sound.
Say the word for each picture.
What beginning sound do you hear?
Write the letter.

harp

hat

jar

kitten

9

quilt

queen

king

jester

Monster Manor!

10

The things in this picture all start with the **l**, **m**, **n**, or **p** sound.
Say the word for each picture.
What beginning sound do you hear?
Write the letter.

net

monkey

puzzle

monster

lizard

11

moon

lollipop

noodles

pizza

Blast Off!

12

The things in this picture all start with the **r**, **s**, or **t** sound.
Say the word for each picture.
What beginning sound do you hear?
Write the letter.

turtle

seal

rocket

snake

13

raccoon

tiger

rabbit

telescope

Wacky Wizard!

14

The things in this picture all start with the **v**, **w**, **x**, **y**, or **z** sound.
Say the word for each picture.
What beginning sound do you hear?
Write the letter.

vase

yo-yo

whistle

vacuum

15

wizard

zebra

zipper

yarn

x-ray

City and Country

16

Say the word for each picture.
If you hear a **hard c** sound, draw a line to the **country**.
If you hear a **soft c** sound, draw a line to the **city**.

country

city

Brain Box

Girl and Giant

17

Say the word for each picture.
If you hear a **hard g** sound, draw a line to the **girl**.
If you hear a **soft g** sound, draw a line to the **giant**.

girl

giant

Brain Bo

Web and Kid

18

The words for these pictures all end in **b** or **d**.
Say the word for each picture.
What ending sound do you hear?
Write the letter.

bird

bread

crib

kid

crab

sled

web

bib

Sun and Swim

19

The things in this picture all end in **m** or **n**.
Say the word for each thing in the picture.
What ending sound do you hear?
Write the letter.

sun

fan

swim

pen

man

clam

drum

Ship and Boat

20

The words for these pictures all end in **p** or **t**.
Say the word for each picture.
What ending sound do you hear?
Write the letter.

ship

boat

net

boot

map

peanut

pot

sheep

Snail and Bus

2

The words for these pictures all end in **l** or **ll**, **s** or **ss**.
Say the word for each picture.
What ending sound do you hear?
Write the letter.

snail

bus

ball

glass

doll

dress

shell

plus

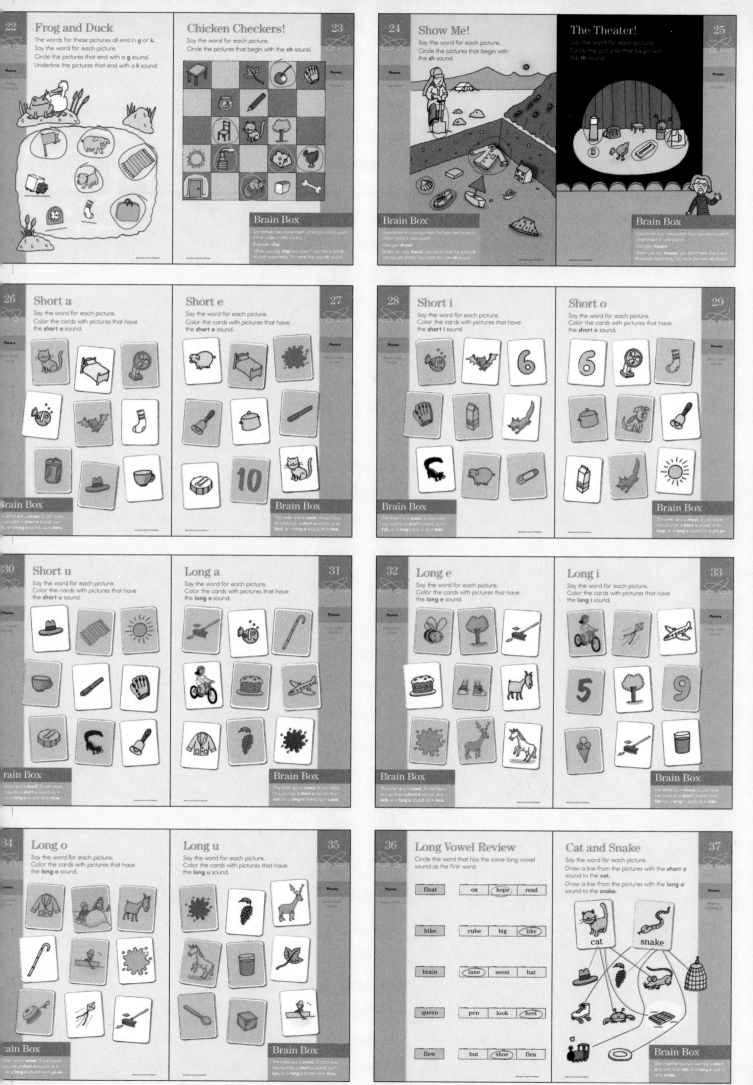

22 Frog and Duck
The words for these pictures all end in **g** or **k**.
Say the word for each picture.
Circle the pictures that end with a **g** sound.
Underline the pictures that end with a **k** sound.

Brain Box

Chicken Checkers! 23
Say the word for each picture.
Circle the pictures that begin with the **ch** sound.

Phonics

Brain Box

24 Show Me!
Say the word for each picture.
Circle the pictures that begin with the **sh** sound.

Phonics

Brain Box

The Theater! 25
Say the word for each picture.
Circle the pictures that begin with the **th** sound.

Phonics

Brain Box

26 Short a
Say the word for each picture.
Color the cards with pictures that have the **short a** sound.

Phonics

Brain Box

Short e 27
Say the word for each picture.
Color the cards with pictures that have the **short e** sound.

Phonics

Brain Box

28 Short i
Say the word for each picture.
Color the cards with pictures that have the **short i** sound.

Phonics

Brain Box

Short o 29
Say the word for each picture.
Color the cards with pictures that have the **short o** sound.

Phonics

Brain Box

30 Short u
Say the word for each picture.
Color the cards with pictures that have the **short u** sound.

Phonics

Brain Box

Long a 31
Say the word for each picture.
Color the cards with pictures that have the **long a** sound.

Phonics

Brain Box

32 Long e
Say the word for each picture.
Color the cards with pictures that have the **long e** sound.

Phonics

Brain Box

Long i 33
Say the word for each picture.
Color the cards with pictures that have the **long i** sound.

Phonics

Brain Box

34 Long o
Say the word for each picture.
Color the cards with pictures that have the **long o** sound.

Phonics

Brain Box

Long u 35
Say the word for each picture.
Color the cards with pictures that have the **long u** sound.

Phonics

Brain Box

36 Long Vowel Review
Circle the word that has the same long vowel sound as the first word.

Phonics

float	ox	hope	read
hike	cube	big	like
brain	lane	seem	bat
queen	pen	look	heel
flew	but	shoe	flea

Cat and Snake 37
Say the word for each picture.
Draw a line from the pictures with the **short a** sound to the cat.
Draw a line from the pictures with the **long a** sound to the snake.

Phonics

cat   snake

Brain Box

54

A Day at the Park

Complete each sentence with a **long i** word from the Word Box.

bike	fly	pie
sky	tie	slide

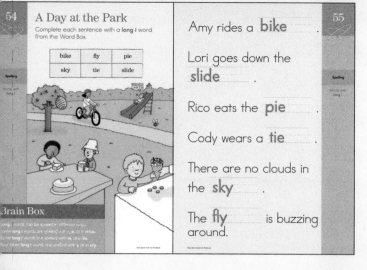

Brain Box

Long i words can be spelled in different ways.
Some **long i** words are spelled with **i_e**, as in **bike**.
Some i words are spelled with **ie**, as in **tie**.
Four other **long i** words are spelled with y, as in sky.

Amy rides a **bike** .

Lori goes down the **slide** .

Rico eats the **pie** .

Cody wears a **tie** .

There are no clouds in the **sky** .

The **fly** is buzzing around.

Backyard Barbecue

Complete each sentence with a **long o** word from the Word Box.

toad	smoke	bone
cone	hose	boat

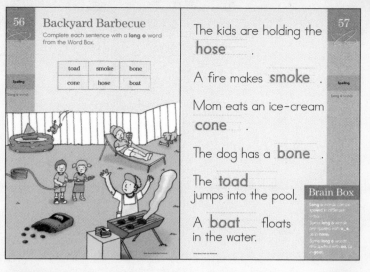

The kids are holding the **hose** .

A fire makes **smoke** .

Mom eats an ice-cream **cone** .

The dog has a **bone** .

The **toad** jumps into the pool.

A **boat** floats in the water.

Brain Box

Long o words can be spelled in different ways.
Some **long o** words are spelled with **o_e**, as in **bone**.
Some long o words are spelled with **oa**, as in **goat**.

Dude Ranch

Complete each sentence with a **long u** word from the Word Box.

mule	stool	tune
room	tooth	boots

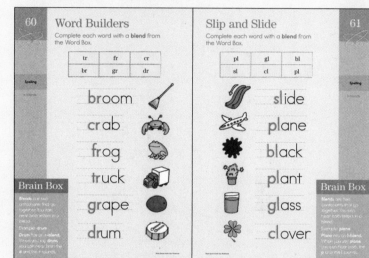

The cowboy **boots** are blue.

Billy hums a **tune** .

The **mule** can carry a heavy load.

The horse's big **tooth** sticks out of his mouth.

Ramón stands on a **stool** .

There are two horses in the **room** .

Brain Box

Long u words can be spelled in different ways.
Some **long u** words are spelled with **u_e**, as in **dude**.
Some long u words are spelled with **oo**, as in **moon**.

Word Builders

Complete each word with a **blend** from the Word Box.

tr	fr	cr
br	gr	dr

broom

crab

frog

truck

grape

drum

Brain Box

Blends are two consonants that go together. You can hear both letters in a blend.
Example: drum
Drum has an **r-blend**. When you say drum, you can hear both the d and the r sounds.

Slip and Slide

Complete each word with a **blend** from the Word Box.

pl	gl	bl
sl	cl	pl

slide

plane

black

plant

glass

clover

Brain Box

Blends are two consonants that go together. You can hear each letter in a blend.
Example: plane
Plane has an **l-blend**. When you say plane, you can hear both the p and the l sounds.

Super S

Complete each word with a **blend** from the Word Box.

sn	sk	sp
sw	st	sm

snail

star

skate

spiral

swing

smile

Brain Box

Blends are two consonants that go together. You can hear both letters in a blend.
Example: snap
Snap has an **s-blend**. When you say snap, you can hear both the s and the n sounds.

64

All About Mike

Read the words on the cards.
Write each word in the correct sentence.

am   and

I   you

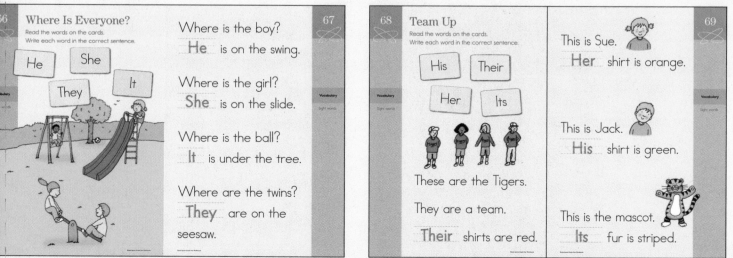

I **am** Mike!

I **like** to read **and** play.

What do **you** like to do?

is   run

see

my

This is **my** dog!

His name **is** Rex.

He likes to **run** .

He must **see** a squirrel.

Where Is Everyone?

Read the words on the cards.
Write each word in the correct sentence.

He   She   They   It

Where is the boy?
He is on the swing.

Where is the girl?
She is on the slide.

Where is the ball?
It is under the tree.

Where are the twins?
They are on the seesaw.

Team Up

Read the words on the cards.
Write each word in the correct sentence.

His   Their   Her   Its

This is Sue.
Her shirt is orange.

This is Jack.
His shirt is green.

This is the mascot.
Its fur is striped.

These are the Tigers.

They are a team.

Their shirts are red.

On the Farm

Read the words on the cards.
Write each word next to the correct animal.

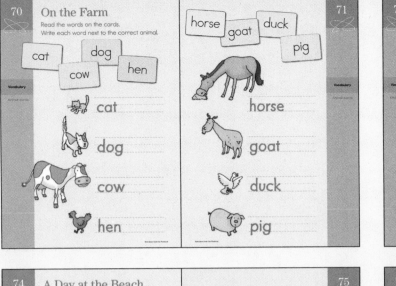

horse goat duck pig

cat dog cow hen

cat

dog

cow

hen

horse

goat

duck

pig

In the Kitchen

Read the words on the cards.
Draw a line from each card to the correct picture on the next page.

bowl

pot

cup

spoon

sink

pan

A Day at the Beach

Read the words on the cards.
Draw a line from each card to the correct picture on the next page.

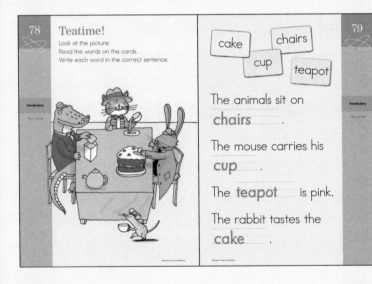

bird

crab

hat

pail

whale

shell

Picnic Party

Read the words on the cards.
Draw a line from each card to the correct picture on the next page.

cheese

apples

corn

hot dogs

salad

juice

pie

Teatime!

Look at the picture.
Read the words on the cards.
Write each word in the correct sentence.

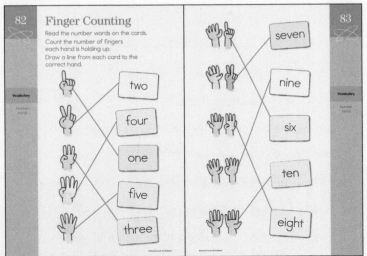

cake chairs cup teapot

The animals sit on
chairs .

The mouse carries his
cup .

The teapot is pink.

The rabbit tastes the
cake .

Color Splash!

Read the color words on the cards.
Color the card the right color.

Write the color word below each color.

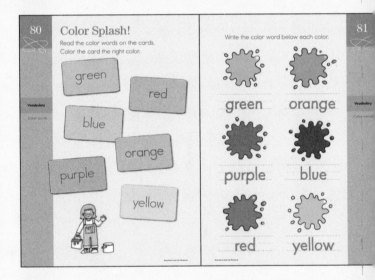

green

red

blue

orange

purple

yellow

green orange

purple blue

red yellow

Finger Counting

Read the number words on the cards.
Count the number of fingers each hand is holding up.
Draw a line from each card to the correct hand.

two

four

one

five

three

seven

nine

six

ten

eight

Activities!

Read the words on the cards.
Write each word in the correct sentence.

dance paint sing read

I like to sing .

I like to paint .

We like to dance .

I like to read .

Soccer Stars!

Read the words on the cards.
Write each word in the correct sentence.

catch kick cheer jog

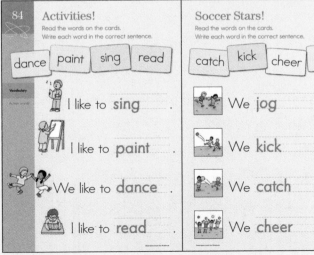

We jog .

We kick .

We catch .

We cheer .

Brain Quest Grade One Workbook

Let's Go!

Read the words on the cards.
Write each word next to the correct picture.

bike bus boat car

car

boat

bike

bus

plane train truck van

plane

truck

train

van

Time to Rhyme!

The words on the cards all rhyme with **brag**.
Write each rhyming word next to the correct picture.

tag wag bag flag

tag

bag

flag

wag

Brain Box

The words on the cards all rhyme with **tan**.
Write each rhyming word next to the correct picture.

can pan man fan

man

fan

can pan

Keep Rhyming!

The words on the cards all rhyme with **cool**.
Write each rhyming word under the correct picture.

stool school spool pool

spool school

pool stool

The words on these cards all rhyme with **tone**.
Write each rhyming word under the correct picture.

bone phone stone cone

bone cone

stone phone

Our Pets

The words on the cards are the pet names.
Each pet's name rhymes with its owner's name.
Complete each sentence with the correct rhyming pet name.

Nate Harry Spike

My name is Larry.
My dog is **Harry**.

My name is Kate.
My cat is **Nate**.

My name is Mike.
My dog is **Spike**.

Bailey Sandy Dan

My name is Hailey.
My dog is **Bailey**.

My name is Andy.
My cat is **Sandy**.

My name is Jan.
My cat is **Dan**.

Find the Rhyme

Say the word for each picture.
Draw a line from each picture to the word it rhymes with.

vest

junk

feel

main

rice

People

Read the **nouns** in the Word Box.
They all name people.
Complete each sentence with the correct **noun** from the Word Box.

| daughter | boy | woman | father | veterinarian |

Brain Box

The **veterinarian** examines the cat.

The **father** is wearing a brown sweater.

His **daughter** has pigtails.

The **boy** has red hair.

The **woman** has a birdcage.

Animals

Read the **nouns** in the Word Box.
They all name animals.

| turtle | cat | bird | dog |

Brain Box

Complete each sentence with the correct **noun** from the Word Box.

The **bird** chirps on a branch.

The **cat** hides behind the bush.

The **dog** walks on a leash.

The **turtle** rests on the rock.

Things

Read the **nouns** in the Word Box.
They all name things.

| hammer | nails | saw | wood |

Brain Box

Complete each sentence with the correct **noun** from the Word Box.

José wants to build a birdhouse.

He has planks of **wood**.

He has a **saw** to cut the wood.

He has a box of **nails**.

The **hammer** is next to his sister.

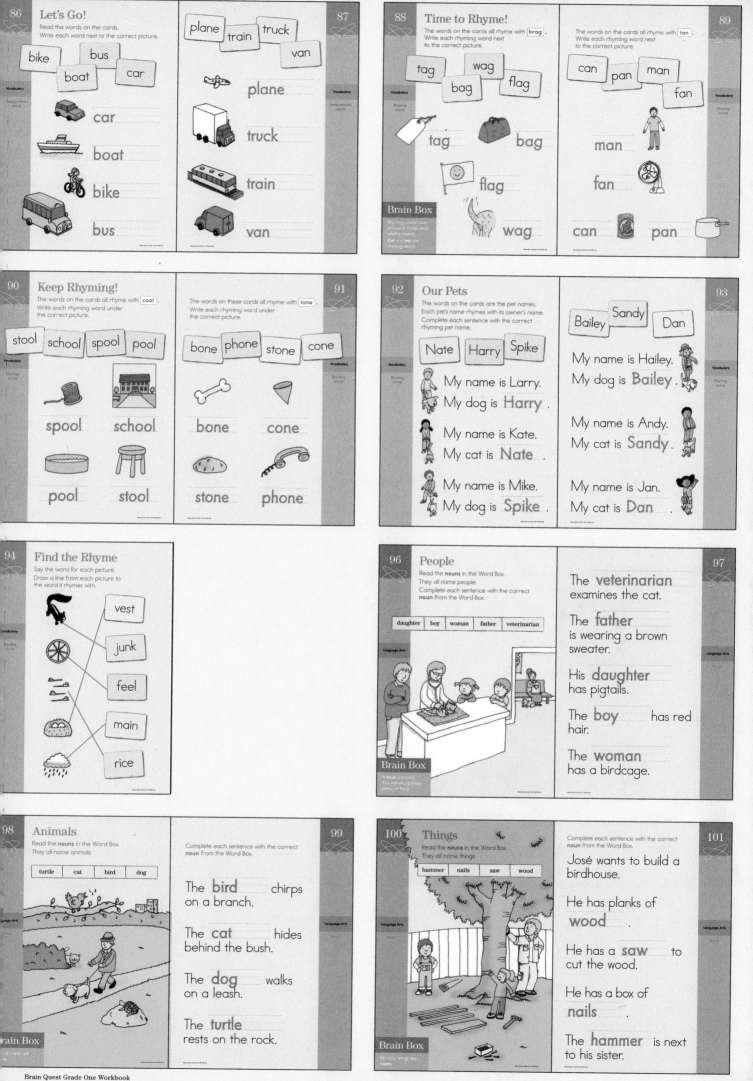

Places

Read the **nouns** in the Word Box.
They all name places.

beach	city	farm
forest	lake	town

Complete each sentence with the correct
noun from the Word Box.

The cow lives on the
farm .

The **forest** has trees.

The boat floats on the
lake .

There are tall buildings
in the **city** .

There is sand on the
beach .

We drive into **town** .

Go, Dino, Go!

Circle the **verb** in each sentence.

The dinosaur (eats).

The dinosaur (hops).

The dinosaur (runs).

The dinosaur (hugs)

The dinosaur (sleeps).

The dinosaur (waves).

Describe It!

Read the **adjectives** in the Word Boxes.
Write the correct **adjective** to tell about each
alien from outer space.

happy	sad	wide

sad

happy

wide

curly	tall	small

small

curly

tall

Describe It!

Read the **adjectives** in the Word Boxes.
Write the correct **adjective** to tell about each
animal.

white	green	gray

The **gray**
elephant lives in
Africa.

The **white**
polar bear lives in
the arctic.

The **green**
lizard lives in the
desert.

pink	brown	red

The **pink**
flamingo lives
near the water.

The **red**
kangaroo lives in
Australia.

The **brown**
deer lives in the
forest.

Cat Chase!

Read this **sentence**:

The (cat) naps.

Circle the **noun**.

Underline the **verb**.

Draw a box around the **capital letter** that
begins the sentence.

Draw a triangle around the **period** that ends
the sentence.

Now copy the **sentence** here.

The cat naps.

Circle the **noun** in this sentence:

The (cat) wakes up.

Underline the **verb** in this sentence:

The cat <u>runs</u>.

Draw a box around the **capital letter** that
begins this sentence:

The dog chases
the cat.

Draw a triangle around the **period**
that ends this sentence:

The dog naps.

Superstar!

These sentences are written wrong.
Write each sentence correctly.

the cow sings.
The cow sings.

the cow dances
The cow dances.

the cow acts
The cow acts.

The receives cow flowers.
**The cow receives
flowers.**

cow bows. The
The cow bows.

waves the cow
The cow waves.

So Many Questions!

These questions are written wrong.
Write each sentence correctly.

how do you feel
How do you feel?

who is your best friend
Who is your best friend?

when is your next show
What is your favorite song?

what is your favorite song
**When is your
next show?**

More Dessert, Please?

Read each **question**.
Circle the question word.

(What) kind of
dessert is it?

(Who) made
the dessert?

(Where) is the dessert?

(When) was the
dessert ready?

(Why) did they make
the dessert?

(How) does it taste?

She Makes Pizza

Add the letter **s** to each verb to tell
what is happening now.

She roll**s** out the
pizza dough.

She pour**s** the
sauce.

She sprinkle**s**
the cheese.

She put**s** the pizza
in the oven.

She take**s** out
the pizza.

They Made a Sundae!

Add the letters **ed** to tell what happened
in the past.

He scoop**ed** the
ice cream.

She pour**ed** the
sauce.

He add**ed** the
bananas.

She spoon**ed**
the nuts.

He look**ed** at
the sundae.

The More the Merrier!
Look at the picture. Complete each sentence using the word **is** or **are**.

The monkeys **are** climbing.

The elephant **is** spraying.

The lions **are** roaring.

The giraffe **is** eating.

The zebra **is** dancing.

The hippos **are** singing.

Farmer's Market
Write the plural for each food word by adding the letter **s** at the end of the word.

pumpkin   pumpkins

pepper   peppers

carrot   carrots

apple   apples

Brain Box

Drake the Dragon
Read about Drake.
Then answer the questions.

This is Drake.
Drake is a dragon.
Drake is purple.
Drake lives in a cave.
Drake lives with a snake.
Drake and the snake are best friends.

What is Drake?
Drake is a **dragon**.

What color is Drake?
Drake is **purple**.

Where does Drake live?
Drake lives in a **cave**.

Who is Drake's best friend?
Drake's best friend is a **snake**.

Picking Apples
Read about apples.
Then answer the questions.

Apples grow on trees.
You can pick apples in the fall.
This family is picking red apples.

Where do apples grow?
Apples grow on **trees**.

When can you pick apples?
You can pick apples in the **fall**.

What color are the apples on the trees?
The apples are **red**.

Camp Out
Read about the camping trip.
Number the pictures from 1 to 4 to show what happens in order.

1. We find a spot by the river.
2. We set up our tents.
3. We get some sticks for a fire.
4. We make dinner and sing!

3

2

4

1

Robot Race
Read about Robbie.
Then answer the questions.

Robbie is a robot.
Robbie is in a race.
Robbie has wheels for feet!
Robbie rolls fast.
He rolls past the other robots.
Robbie wins the race!

What is Robbie?
Robbie is a **robot**.

What does Robbie have for feet?
Robbie has **wheels**.

Who wins the race?
Robbie wins the race.

Draw your own robot here!

A Big Day
Read the sentences.
Choose the correct feeling word to tell how each person feels. Write it on the line.

Mario can't wait to get to the zoo.

Mario is **excited**.

| excited | angry |

Kate's kite is stuck in a tree!

Kate is **upset**.

| upset | happy |

Steve doesn't know anyone at the party.

Steve is **shy**.

| silly | shy |

Marty lost his dog.

Marty is **sad**.

| sad | sleepy |

Marty found his dog!

Marty is **glad**.

| mad | glad |

Luis played a long game of baseball.

Luis is **tired**.

| tired | frightened |

Plants!
Read about plants.

Flowers are plants.
Trees are plants.
Grass is a plant, too.
Rocks are not plants.
Water is not a plant.
The rabbit is not a plant.

Color the cards with plant words green.

rocks

rabbit

trees

grass

flowers

water

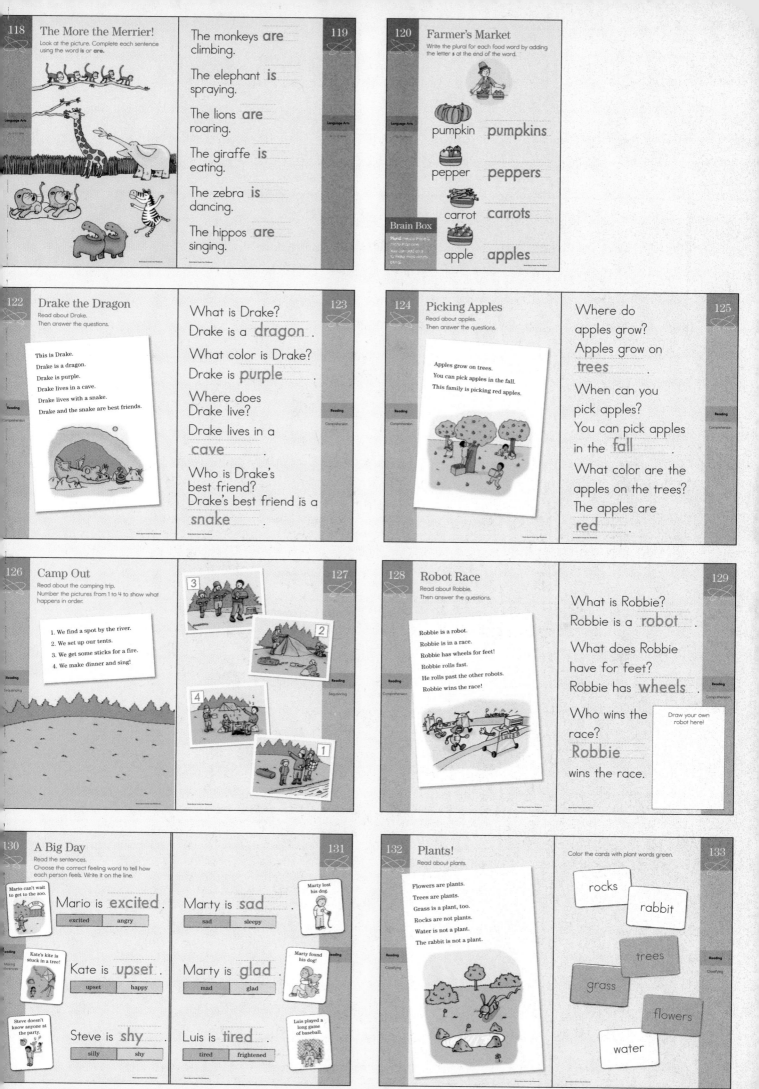

134 — Allie the Alien

Read about Allie.

Allie has strong eyes.
Allie sees lots of things on Earth.
She sees land.
She sees water.
She sees animals.
Allie sees you, too!

135

What does Allie see on Earth? Write it on the lines.

She sees land.
She sees water.
She sees animals.
She sees me !

Send a postcard to Allie.
Draw a picture of yourself saying hello!

136 — Monster Music!

Read each sentence.
Then draw a line to the matching picture.

Molly plays the drums.

Michael plays the tuba.

Mark plays the violin.

Maria plays the flute.

138 — The Witch's Spell

Read about the witch.
Number the pictures from 1 to 5 to show what happens in order.

1. Wilma the Witch has a frog.
2. She turns the frog into a bird!
3. She turns the bird into a bug!
4. She turns the bug into a dog!
5. She turns the dog into a frog again.

139

142 — Doggy Diary

Complete each sentence with a word from the Word Box.
Then copy the whole sentence on the blank.

| bark | happy | stick | Gus | fetch |

My name is Gus
My name is Gus.

I like to fetch .
I like to fetch.

143

I fetch a stick .
I fetch a stick.

I like to bark .
I like to bark.

I am a happy dog.
I am a happy dog.

146 — Playing at the Pond

Write a sentence about each animal you see at the pond. Begin each sentence with **I see a**.

frog
fox
duck

I see a duck.
I see a frog.
I see a fox.

147

deer
fish
turtle

Brain Box
A statement is a sentence that explains or tells what someone or something does. A statement begins with a capital letter and ends with a period.

I see a deer.
I see a fish.
I see a turtle.

148 — Let's Ride!

Write a sentence about each way to ride.
Begin each sentence with **I ride in a**.

boat
car

I ride in a car.
I ride in a boat.

149

plane
train
wagon

I ride in a plane.
I ride in a train.
I ride in a wagon.

150 — Silly Pig!

Complete each sentence with the correct word from the Word Box.
Copy the whole sentence on the blank.

| silly | sad | angry |

The pig is silly .
The pig is silly.

| house | tree | mud |

The pig rolls in mud .
The pig rolls in mud.

| runs | dances | sits |

The pig dances
The pig dances.

151

| eats | sleeps | sings |

The pig eats
The pig eats.

| dog | cat | girl |

The pig likes the girl
The pig likes the girl.

| ice cream | pizza | cookies |

They eat ice cream
They eat ice cream.

162 — Up, Up, and Away!

Number the pictures from 1 to 4 to show what happens in order.

163 — Welcome to the Club!

Number the pictures from 1 to 4 to show what happens in order.

Dog Wash

Number the pictures from 1 to 4 to show what happens in order.

Sequencing and Sorting
Sequencing

Lunchtime!

Number the pictures from 1 to 6 to show what happens in order.

Sequencing and Sorting
Sequencing

A Chick Is Born

Draw a line from each picture to the correct number on the time line to show what happens in order.

Sequencing and Sorting
Sequencing

| 1 | 2 | 3 |

| 4 | 5 | 6 |

Growing Tall!

Draw a line from each picture to the correct number on the time line to show what happens in order.

Sequencing and Sorting
Sequencing

| 1 | 2 | 3 |

Sequencing and Sorting
Sequencing

| 4 | 5 | 6 |

Search and Sort

Look at the **numbers** in the clouds. Write them in **numerical order** below the balloon.

8
5
2
10
7

NUMBERS

2, 5, 7, 8, 10

Sequencing and Sorting
Sorting

Look at the **letters** in the clouds. Write them in **alphabetical order** below the balloon.

t
p
a
z
i

LETTERS

a, i, p, t, z

Sequencing and Sorting
Sorting

Sorting Shapes

Draw a line to match the things to the shapes.

Sequencing and Sorting
Sorting

Shopping Sort

Draw a line to put each thing in the correct shopping basket below.

FOOD   CLOTHES   SCHOOL SUPPLIES

Sequencing and Sorting
Sorting

Moving Day

Draw a line from the box to the matching number of things.

1
2
3
4
5

Math Skills
Number recognition

6
7
8
9
10

Math Skills
Number recognition

Count Dracula!

Fill in the missing numbers. Go across and write the numbers in order.

1	2	3	4	5	6	7	8	9	10
11	12	13	14	15	16	17	18	19	20
21	22	23	24	25	26	27	28	29	30
31	32	33	34	35	36	37	38	39	40
41	42	43	44	45	46	47	48	49	50
51	52	53	54	55	56	57	58	59	60
61	62	63	64	65	66	67	68	69	70
71	72	73	74	75	76	77	78	79	80
81	82	83	84	85	86	87	88	89	90
91	92	93	94	95	96	97	98	99	100

Math Skills
Counting to 100

Counting Crayons

Write the number of crayons below each group.

2   4

6   8

10   12

Now say the numbers out loud. You are counting by 2s!

Math Skills

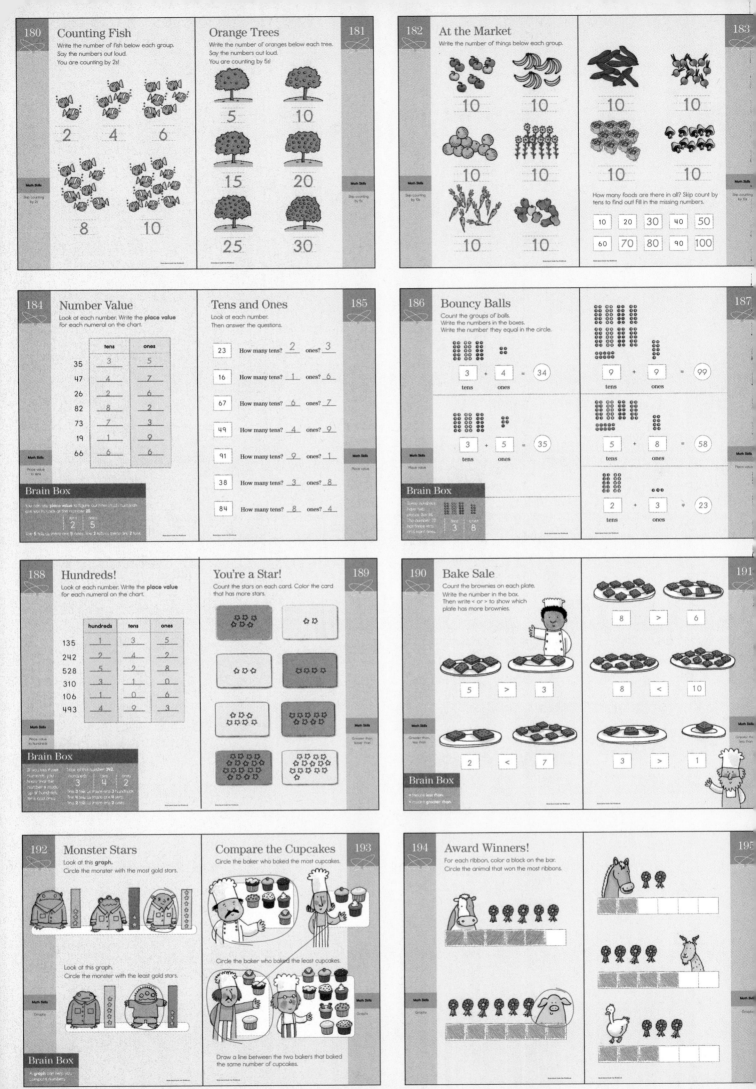

180 Counting Fish
Write the number of fish below each group.
Say the numbers out loud.
You are counting by 2s!

2 4 6
8 10

Orange Trees 181
Write the number of oranges below each tree.
Say the numbers out loud.
You are counting by 5s!

5 10
15 20
25 30

182 At the Market
Write the number of things below each group.

10 10
10 10
10 10

183

10 10
10 10

How many foods are there in all? Skip count by tens to find out! Fill in the missing numbers.

| 10 | 20 | 30 | 40 | 50 |
| 60 | 70 | 80 | 90 | 100 |

184 Number Value
Look at each number. Write the **place value** for each numeral on the chart.

	tens	ones
35	3	5
47	4	7
26	2	6
82	8	2
73	7	3
19	1	9
66	6	6

Brain Box

Tens and Ones 185
Look at each number.
Then answer the questions.

23 How many tens? 2 ones? 3
16 How many tens? 1 ones? 6
67 How many tens? 6 ones? 7
49 How many tens? 4 ones? 9
91 How many tens? 9 ones? 1
38 How many tens? 3 ones? 8
84 How many tens? 8 ones? 4

186 Bouncy Balls
Count the groups of balls.
Write the numbers in the boxes.
Write the number they equal in the circle.

3 + 4 = 34
tens ones

3 + 5 = 35
tens ones

187

9 + 9 = 99
tens ones

5 + 8 = 58
tens ones

2 + 3 = 23
tens ones

Brain Box

188 Hundreds!
Look at each number. Write the **place value** for each numeral on the chart.

	hundreds	tens	ones
135	1	3	5
242	2	4	2
528	5	2	8
310	3	1	0
106	1	0	6
493	4	9	3

Brain Box

You're a Star! 189
Count the stars on each card. Color the card that has more stars.

190 Bake Sale
Count the brownies on each plate.
Write the number in the box.
Then write < or > to show which plate has more brownies.

5 > 3
2 < 7

191
8 > 6
8 < 10
3 > 1

Brain Box

192 Monster Stars
Look at this **graph**.
Circle the monster with the most gold stars.

Look at this graph.
Circle the monster with the least gold stars.

Brain Box
A graph can help you compare numbers.

Compare the Cupcakes 193
Circle the baker who baked the most cupcakes.

Circle the baker who baked the least cupcakes.

Draw a line between the two bakers that baked the same number of cupcakes.

194 Award Winners!
For each ribbon, color a block on the bar.
Circle the animal that won the most ribbons.

195

Book Worm

How many books do you think you see?
Don't count them. Just take a guess!

Write the number
you guessed:

Good job! You estimated!
Now count the books.
Write the number you counted: 19
Were you close?

Pot of Gold

How many gold coins do you think you see?
Don't count them. Just take a guess!

Write the number you guessed:

Good job! You estimated!
Now count the coins.
Write the number you counted: 23
Were you close?

Snow Day!

How many snowflakes do you think you
see? Don't count them. Just take a guess!
Write the number you guessed:

Now count the snowflakes.
Write the number you counted: 16
Were you close?

Play Ball!

Count the balls in each group.
Write the number in the box below.
Write the **sum** in the last box.

$3 + 2 = 5$

$1 + 3 = 4$

$5 + 3 = 8$

Brain Box

Star Search

Count the stars in each group.
Write the number in the box below.
Write the **sum** in the last box.

$2 + 6 = 8$

$5 + 4 = 9$

$7 + 1 = 8$

At the Toy Store

Count the toys in each group.
Write the number in the box below.
Add the numbers. Write the **sum** in the last box.

$5 + 3 = 8$

$4 + 2 = 6$

$6 + 1 = 7$

$7 + 5 = 12$

$3 + 4 = 7$

$1 + 2 = 3$

Super Scoops!

Count the scoops on each cone.
Write the number in the box.
Add the numbers to find out how many scoops
there are in all.
Write the **sum** in the box below the line.

4
+ 3
———
7

5
+ 2
———
7

Brain Box

Pancake Party!

Count the pancakes on each plate.
Write each number in the box.
Add the numbers to find out how many
pancakes there are in all.
Write the **sum** in the box below the line.

6
+ 7
———
13

5
+ 10
———
15

So Many Shells!

Count the shells in each group.
Add the shells.
Draw a line to the correct answer.

10

5

4

7

Monster Math

Add the numbers in the boxes.
Write the **sum** in the box.

$3 + 5 = 8$

$2 + 4 = 6$

$8 + 1 = 9$

$2 + 3 = 5$

$6 + 1 = 7$

Dragon Math

Add the numbers.
Write the **sum** in each box.

$5 + 2 = 7$

$4 + 8 = 12$

$1 + 9 = 10$

$2 + 8 = 10$

6
+ 1
———
7

3
+ 5
———
8

6
+ 4
———
10

2
+ 4
———
6

$1 + 6 = 7$

$2 + 7 = 9$

$5 + 6 = 11$

$9 + 5 = 14$

$4 + 3 = 7$

2
+ 4
———
6

5
+ 7
———
12

11
+ 4
———
15

4
+ 7
———
11

$7 + 5 = 12$

$4 + 8 = 12$

$7 + 6 = 13$

$10 + 3 = 13$

$5 + 5 = 10$

Bear Numbers

Add the numbers.
Write the **sum** in each box.

$6 + 4 = 10$

$3 + 2 = 5$

$7 + 7 = 14$

$2 + 6 = 8$

5
+ 12
———
17

3
+ 7
———
10

2
+ 9
———
11

3
+ 9
———
12

$3 + 2 = 5$

$4 + 7 = 11$

$7 + 2 = 9$

$3 + 9 = 12$

$9 + 2 = 11$

$4 + 1 = 5$

$5 + 4 = 9$

6
+ 2
———
8

5
+ 3
———
8

8
+ 1
———
9

1
+ 8
———
9

$8 + 4 = 12$

$2 + 10 = 12$

$4 + 10 = 14$

$5 + 6 = 11$

$10 + 4 = 14$

Terrific 20!

Count the insects in each group.
Write the number in the box below.
Add the numbers.
Write the **sum** in the box.

$10 + 10 = 20$

$5 + 15 = 20$

$12 + 8 = 20$

$4 + 16 = 20$

$7 + 13 = 20$

$9 + 11 = 20$

Take a Slice!

Count the slices in each pizza.
Count the number of slices taken away.
Write the number of slices that are left.

Brain Box

To subtract you take away. For example: $3 - 2 = 1$. Here, we are subtracting the number 2 from the number 3. We use a − sign to show the number we have left. We call the **difference**. We can put a sign to show the difference.

$6 - 2 = 4$

$5 - 2 = 3$

Balloon Pop

Count the balloons.
Count the balloons that have flown away.
Write how many are left.

$4 - 2 = 2$

$8 - 4 = 4$

$7 - 5 = 2$

Let's Bowl!

Count how many pins are standing.
Count how many pins fall.
Subtract to tell how many pins are left.

$10 - 3 = 7$

$7 - 4 = 3$

$9 - 5 = 4$

Doggy Dessert

Count the dog bones.
Count how many bones the dog eats.
Subtract to tell how many bones are left.

$6 - 2 = 4$

$6 - 4 = 2$

$9 - 2 = 7$

Falling Leaves

Count the leaves.
Count how many leaves fly away.
Subtract to tell how many are left.

15
$- 10$
5

12
$- 4$
8

Brain Box

Subtraction problems can be written two ways.

Shooting Stars

Count the stars in the sky.
Count how many stars shoot away.
Subtract to tell how many stars are left.
Write the numbers on the lines.

8
$- 5$
3

6
$- 4$
2

Go in the Snow!

Subtract the numbers.
Write the **difference** in the box.

$10 - 5 = 5$

$5 - 2 = 3$

$12 - 2 = 10$

$3 - 1 = 2$

$7 - 1 = 6$ $5 - 2 = 3$

$5 - 3 = 2$ $10 - 3 = 7$

$9 - 5 = 4$ $7 - 6 = 1$

$8 - 2 = 6$ $9 - 8 = 1$

$4 - 2 = 2$ $4 - 3 = 1$

8	6	7	7
-4	-3	-4	-3
4	3	3	4

2	4	8	10
-1	-4	-4	-5
1	0	4	5

The Magic Word

Add or **subtract** the numbers.
Write the answers in the boxes.

$7 + 13 = 20$ O $10 - 5 = 5$ E

$8 - 7 = 1$ P $12 - 8 = 4$ R

6
$+ 4$
10 S

20
$- 5$
15 T

Figure out the wizard's magic word. Write the
letters that match the numbers in the boxes.

1	4	5	10	15	20
P	R	E	S	T	O

Balloon Blowup!

Look at the shapes of the balloons.

Color the rectangles yellow.

Color the diamonds purple.

Color the ovals pink.

Color the circles red.

Color the squares blue.

Color the triangles green.

Tell My Fortune!

Color the triangle purple.
Color the rectangle **brown**.
Color the circle gray.
Color the diamond green.
Color the ovals blue.

Quiz Me!

Answer the questions about shapes.

How many sides does a square have?   **4**

How many corners does a diamond have?   **4**

How many sides does a triangle have?   **3**

How many corners does a circle have?   **0**

How many corners does a rectangle have?   **4**

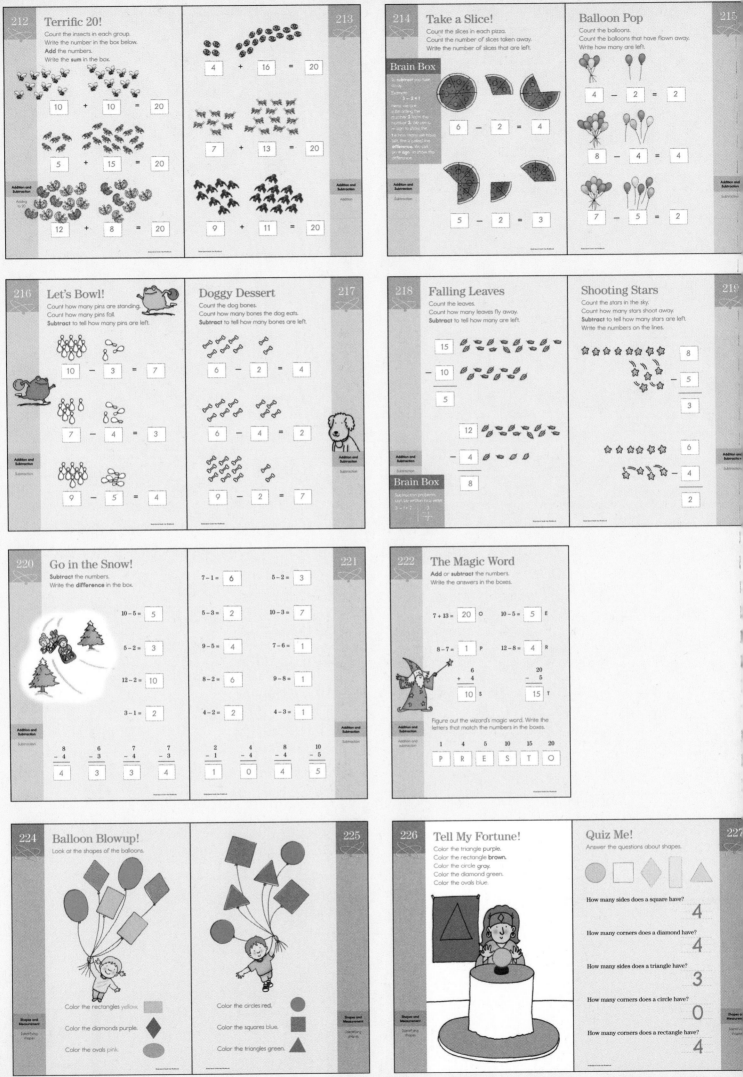

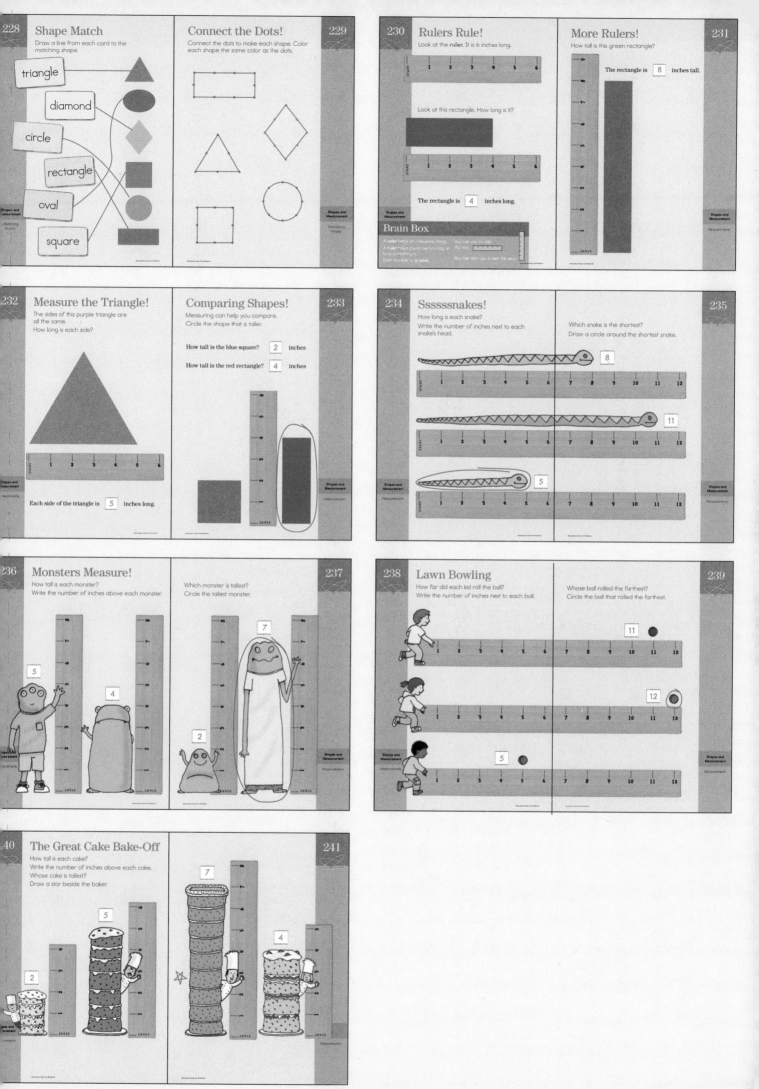

228 Shape Match

Draw a line from each card to the matching shape.

triangle

diamond

circle

rectangle

oval

square

Connect the Dots! 229

Connect the dots to make each shape. Color each shape the same color as the dots.

230 Rulers Rule!

Look at the **ruler.** It is 6 inches long.

Look at this rectangle. How long is it?

The rectangle is [4] inches long.

Brain Box

A **ruler** helps you measure things. A ruler helps you know how big or long something is. Each number is an **inch**.

You can use a ruler this way.

You can also use a ruler the way.

More Rulers! 231

How tall is this green rectangle?

The rectangle is [8] inches tall.

232 Measure the Triangle!

The sides of this purple triangle are all the same.
How long is each side?

Each side of the triangle is [5] inches long.

Comparing Shapes! 233

Measuring can help you compare.
Circle the shape that is taller.

How tall is the blue square? [2] inches

How tall is the red rectangle? [4] inches

234 Sssssssnakes!

How long is each snake?
Write the number of inches next to each snake's head.

[8]

[11]

[5]

Which snake is the shortest?
Draw a circle around the shortest snake. 235

236 Monsters Measure!

How tall is each monster?
Write the number of inches above each monster.

[5]

[4]

Which monster is tallest?
Circle the tallest monster. 237

[7]

[2]

238 Lawn Bowling

How far did each kid roll the ball?
Write the number of inches next to each ball.

[11]

[12]

[5]

Whose ball rolled the farthest?
Circle the ball that rolled the farthest. 239

240 The Great Cake Bake-Off

How tall is each cake?
Write the number of inches above each cake.
Whose cake is tallest?
Draw a star beside the baker.

[2]

[5]

[7]

[4]

241

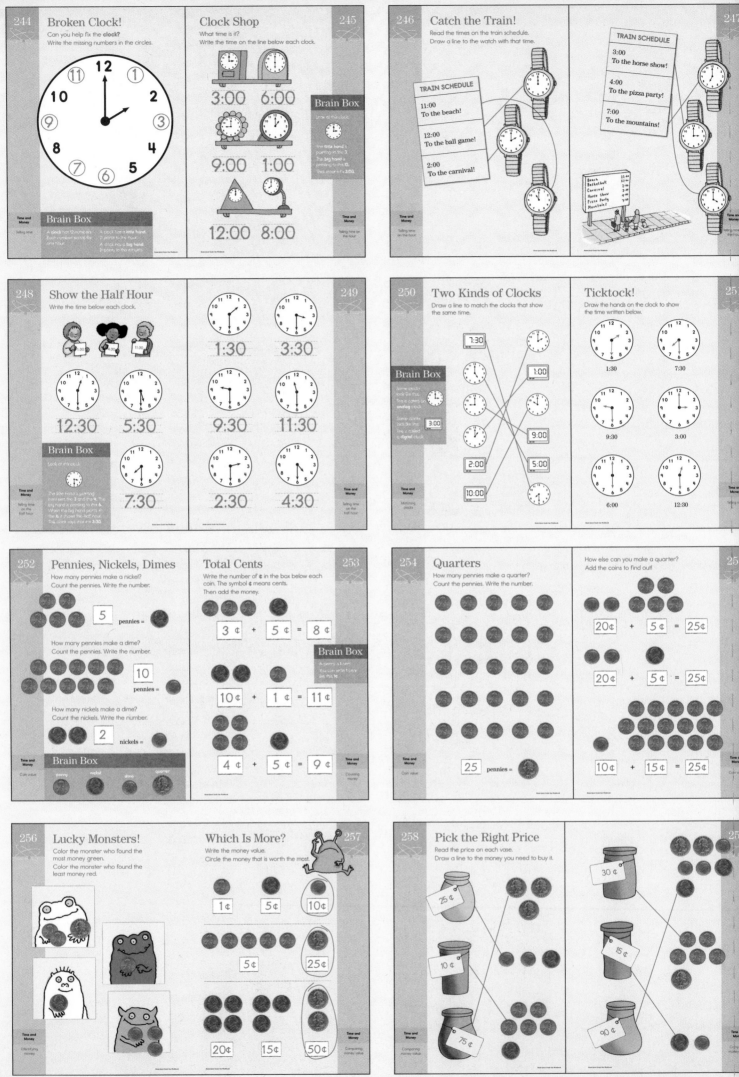

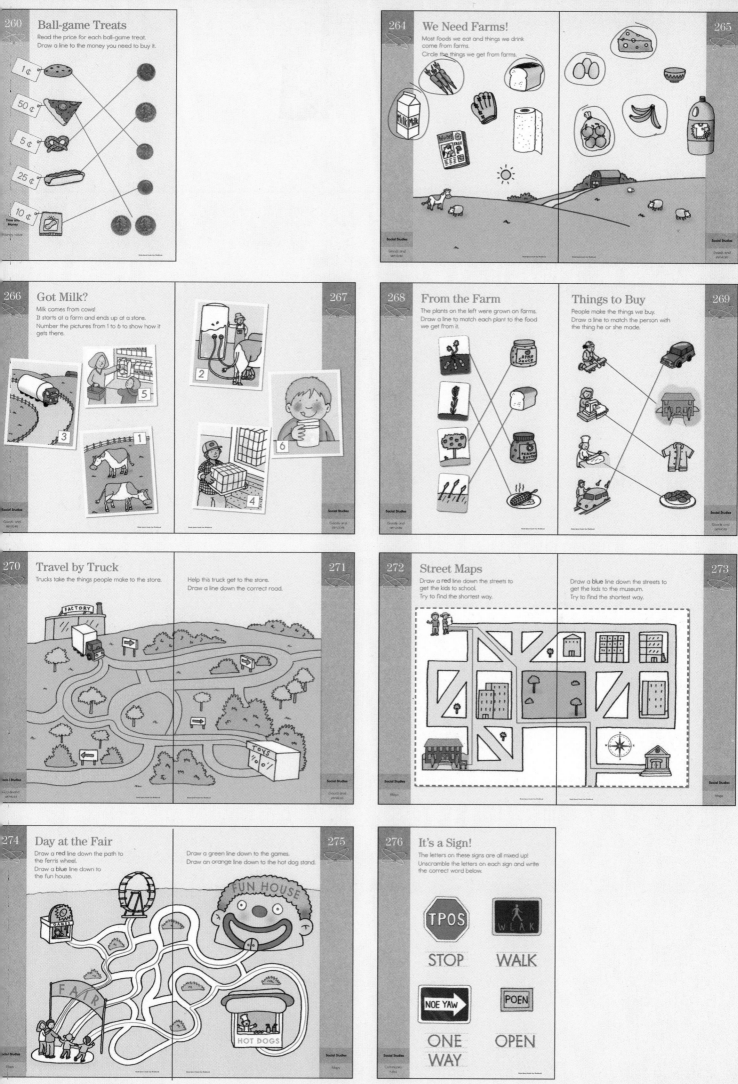

Ball-game Treats

Read the price for each ball-game treat.
Draw a line to the money you need to buy it.

1¢

50¢

5¢

25¢

10¢

Time and Money

Money value

We Need Farms!

Most foods we eat and things we drink come from farms.
Circle the things we get from farms.

Milk

Social Studies
Goods and services

Social Studies
Goods and services

Got Milk?

Milk comes from cows!
It starts at a farm and ends up at a store.
Number the pictures from 1 to 6 to show how it gets there.

5

2

3

1

6

4

Social Studies
Goods and services

Social Studies
Goods and services

From the Farm

The plants on the left were grown on farms.
Draw a line to match each plant to the food we get from it.

APPLE SAUCE

PEANUT BUTTER

Things to Buy

People make the things we buy.
Draw a line to match the person with the thing he or she made.

Social Studies
Goods and services

Social Studies
Goods and services

Travel by Truck

Trucks take the things people make to the store.

Help this truck get to the store.
Draw a line down the correct road.

FACTORY

TOYS

Social Studies
Goods and services

Social Studies
Goods and services

Street Maps

Draw a **red** line down the streets to get the kids to school.
Try to find the shortest way.

Draw a **blue** line down the streets to get the kids to the museum.
Try to find the shortest way.

Social Studies
Maps

Social Studies
Maps

Day at the Fair

Draw a **red** line down the path to the ferris wheel.
Draw a **blue** line down to the fun house.

Draw a **green** line down to the games.
Draw an **orange** line down to the hot dog stand.

FUN HOUSE

FAIR

GAMES

HOT DOGS

Social Studies
Maps

Social Studies
Maps

It's a Sign!

The letters on these signs are all mixed up!
Unscramble the letters on each sign and write the correct word below.

TPOS

STOP

WLAK

WALK

NOE YAW

ONE WAY

POEN

OPEN

Social Studies
Community rules

278 Our Earth

Read about the Earth. On the globe below, color all the land parts brown. Color all the water parts blue.

Earth is the planet we live on.
It has land and water.

land
water
land
water
land

The Sun 279

Read about the sun.
Write the answers to the questions on the lines below.

The sun is a star.

The sun is very important.

It gives us light.

It gives us heat.

Without the sun, we could not survive.

The earth travels around the sun once per year.

This is called an orbit.

Is the sun a moon or a star?

The sun is a star.

What does the sun give us?

Light and heat.

280 Night and Day

Read about night and day. Write the answers to the questions on the lines below.

Earth spins as it orbits around the sun.

When Earth is facing the sun, it is day.

The sun shines on Earth during the day, so it is light.

When Earth is facing away from the sun, it is night.

The sun doesn't shine on Earth at night, so it is dark.

What does Earth do as it orbits around the sun?

The Earth spins.

When Earth faces the sun, is it day or night?

It is day.

The Seasons 281

Look at each picture.
Write the season name below the picture.
Use the words from the Word Box.

winter	spring	summer	fall

summer   fall

spring   winter

282 Lots of Weather

Look at each picture.
Describe the weather in each picture using a word from the Word Box.

sunny	rainy	snowy	windy

rainy   sunny

windy   snowy

284 Plants and the Sun

Find the plants in the picture.
Color them green.

Plant Life Cycles 285

Number the pictures from 1 to 6 to show the life cycle of an apple tree.

All living things follow a life cycle.

They are born.

They grow.

They reproduce.

They die.

3   5   2

6   4   1

286 Butterfly Life Cycle

Read about the butterfly's life cycle.
Then label each stage of the life cycle on the picture.

A butterfly is an insect. All insects follow a life cycle.

First, a butterfly lays an egg.

The egg hatches into a caterpillar.

After eating a lot, the caterpillar spins a chrysalis.

Inside the chrysalis, the caterpillar turns into an adult.

Soon, the adult emerges, or comes out, from the chrysalis.

A new butterfly is born!

egg   caterpillar

chrysalis   butterfly

288 Solids and Liquids

Read about solids and liquids.
Write the letter **S** below the solid things.
Write the letter **L** below the liquid things.

Some things are solid.

Solids do not change their shape.

Some things are liquid.

Liquids can change shape.

L   S   S   L

L   S   L   S

It's Good to Recycle! 289

Read about recycling.
Circle the things at this party that can be recycled.

We can turn old things into new things.

This is called recycling.

We can recycle cans.

We can recycle paper.

We can recycle bottles.

290 Drop It in the Bin

Look at the picture on each bin.
Draw a line from all the things you can recycle to the correct bin.

PLASTIC   PAPER   CANS

Brain Quest Extras

Congratulations!

You've finished the Brain Quest Workbook!
In this section, you'll find:

Brain Quest Mini-Deck

Cut out the cards and make your own Brain Quest deck.

Play by yourself or with a friend.

Brainiac Certificate

Put a sticker on each square for every chapter you complete. Finish the whole workbook, and you're an official Brainiac!

And don't forget to turn to the end of the workbook. You'll find stickers and a 100 Creatures poster!

Questions

Order these numbers from smallest to largest: 77, 25, 59, 30.

Which word doesn't belong here: horse, cow, tree, pig?

What 3 numbers come just after 38?

"I like your green shoes." How many words are in this sentence?

Questions

What number is in the tens place in 146?

Say the words that begin with the same sounds: good, junk, gerbil.

Which month has more days: January or February?

Which word is the verb: "Milly drove the car to the store"?

Questions

Janet plays soccer every Tuesday and Thursday. How many weekdays does she play?

How do you spell the number 7?

Which activity takes about 15 minutes: eating breakfast or washing your hands?

Which word means the same as "leave": depart or demand?

Questions

If 5 + 3 equals 8, what does 8 – 5 equal?

What letter don't you say in the word spelled w–r–i–s–t?

Is 12 an even number or an odd number?

What word should you leave out of this command: "You sit down"?

Questions

Both sides of a symmetrical capital letter look alike. Find the symmetrical capital letter: R, K, S, A

Fix this sentence: "Give the basket to I, please."

The time on the clock is 1:20. What number does the minute hand point to?

Put these parts of a story in the right order: end, beginning, middle.

Questions

What is the sum of 14 plus 10?

Which comes first in alphabetical order: carrot, lettuce, broccoli?

What 5 coins add up to a nickel?

How do you change the word "toy" to make it mean more than one?

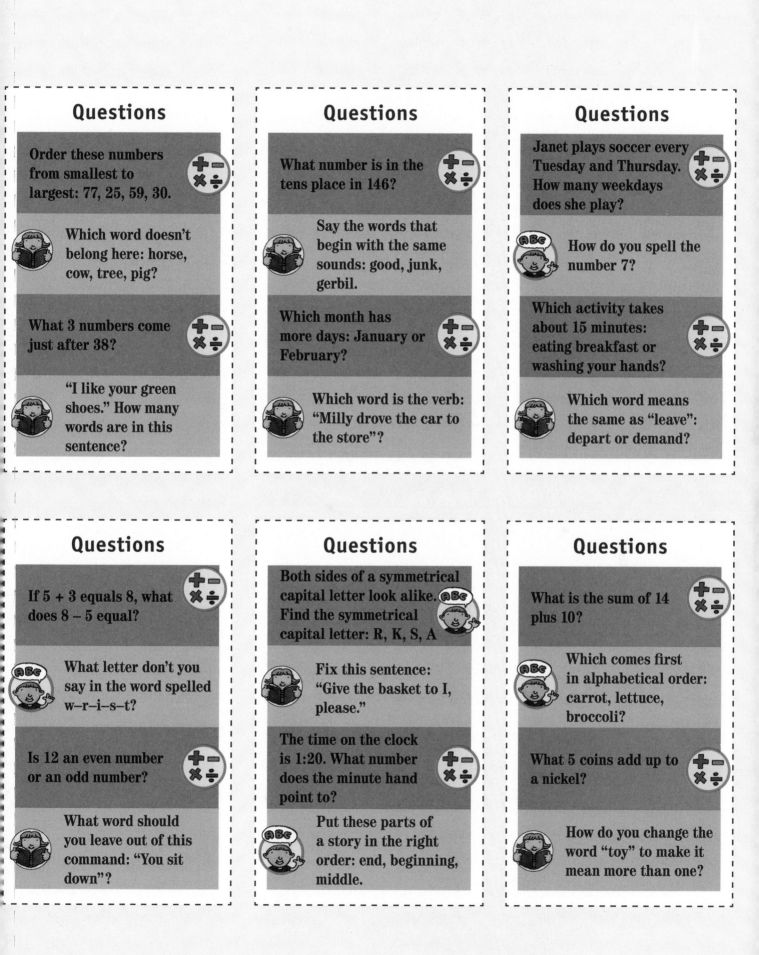

Answers

2 weekdays

s–e–v–e–n (seven)

eating breakfast

depart

Answers

4

junk, gerbil

January (it has 31 days; February has 28, or 29 in a leap year)

drove

Answers

25, 30, 59, 77

tree (it's not an animal)

39, 40, 41

5

Answers

24

broccoli

5 pennies (1¢+ 1¢ + 1¢ + 1¢ + 1¢ = 5¢)

Add the letter "s." (toys)

Answers

A

"Give the basket to me, please."

the 4

beginning, middle, end

Answers

3

w

an even number

"You"

Questions

Two dancers make one pair. How many dancers will make 3 pairs?

What three-letter word can you make from these letters: h–e–s?

The table has four sides. Is it a square or a triangle?

What's the opposite of "hot"?

Questions

In 15 minutes, it will be 2:45. What time is it now?

Which is a sentence?
1. A happy dream.
2. Mara is dreaming.

Counting by tens, which number comes next: 30, 40, 50, …?

Fix the verb in this sentence: "She's gonna go to school today."

Questions

Which does NOT add up to 9: 2 + 5, 1 + 8, 5 + 4?

"What time is it?" Is this a question or a statement?

Every sandwich has two slices of cheese. Elsa ate two sandwiches. How many slices of cheese did she eat in all?

Which place comes first in alphabetical order: school, home, bakery?

Questions

Mercedes took 7 apples and 6 oranges. Daniel took 6 apples and 4 oranges. Who took more apples?

Which noun names a person: classroom, teaching, teacher?

What is the sum of 12 + 13?

What's a longer way to say "I'm feeling tired"?

Questions

What does the minus sign (–) tell you to do?

Which word is spelled with one "e": bee or the?

It's 6:30. What time will it be in one hour?

Fix the mistake: "Yesterday I go to a party."

Questions

Which is longer: 1 minute or 1 hour?

Fix this sentence: "Vivian is the most happy girl in school."

What three numbers come between 28 and 32?

What is the fifth letter of the alphabet?

Answers

2 + 5 (2 + 5 = 7)

a question

4 (2 + 2 = 4)

bakery

Answers

2:30

2. (A sentence tells a complete idea.)

60

She's <u>going to</u> go to school today.

Answers

6 dancers

she

a square

cold

Answers

1 hour (there are 60 minutes in 1 hour)

"Vivian is the happiest girl in school."

29, 30, 31

E

Answers

subtract

The

7:30

Yesterday I <u>went</u> to a party.

Answers

Mercedes (7 + 6 = 13 and 6 + 4 = 10. 13 is more than 10.)

teacher

25

<u>I am</u> feeling tired.

Questions

Add 4 + 5 + 2. What's the sum?

Which words in this sentence rhyme: "My favorite hat is the flat one."

What four numbers come right before 46?

Spell the opposite of "sister."

Questions

It's 12:30. What time will it be in one hour?

Which letter goes in front of "a–t" to spell the word for a mouse-chasing pet?

When you subtract 4 from 9 to get 5, which number is the difference?

"i have seven french dolls." Which words in this sentence need a capital letter?

Questions

When I'm added to 12, the total is 20. What number am I?

Is a sparrow a fish, a bird, or an insect?

If you cut a pie into 10 pieces, and give 4 pieces away, how many pieces do you have left?

Which is an animal: house, horse, forest, cloud?

Questions

There are 12 eggs in a dozen. How many eggs are in half a dozen?

Find another word for a chair: heat, peat, seat, feet.

Which shape is round: square, circle, triangle?

Find the pronoun: "She is wearing a nice shirt."

Questions

Avery saw 3 birds in the tree. Monica saw 1 more. How many wings did they see in all?

Which word needs a capital letter: "I like to visit Grandma in florida"?

Which letter comes next: DRD, DRD, DRD, …?

What's the opposite of "tall"?

Questions

Is 15 greater than 13 by 2, 3, or 5?

Which are the rhyming words: blue, do, show?

What two coins add up to a dime?

Which comes first in a dictionary: dragon or lion?

Answers

8 (12 + 8 = 20)

a bird

6

horse

Answers

1:30

c (cat)

5

"I" and "French"

Answers

11

hat, flat

42, 43, 44, 45

b–r–o–t–h–e–r
(brother)

Answers

2 (15 − 13 = 2)

blue and do

2 nickels
(5¢ + 5¢ = 10¢)

dragon

Answers

8 wings (2 + 2 + 2 + 2)

Florida

D

short

Answers

6

seat

circle

she

Questions

Which two numbers are closest to 40: 35, 42, 51?

"My hands are warm but my nose is cold." Which words mean the opposite?

How many pieces of clothing are in the closet: 3 shirts, 2 pairs of pants, 1 dress?

Which is NOT a month: March, February, October, Thursday?

Questions

Which capital letter has a horizontal line: M, C, H?

I say "woof." My name rhymes with "log." What am I?

You have 3 groups of 5. What's your total?

What do you call a baby sheep?

Questions

If 14 minus 7 equals 7, what does 15 minus 7 equal?

Which comes first in a dictionary: wind or rain?

How much is 6 + 6?

Which words begin with the same sound: photo, potato, final?

Questions

You have 6 groups of 10. What number do you have?

What's a shorter way to say "This playground does not have a slide"?

There is one bicycle and two unicycles. How many wheels in all?

What word can you add to "news" to name a thing you read?

Questions

Which is smallest: a flower, a bush, or a tree?

Find the pronoun in this sentence: "Ricardo gave Sun his jacket."

How many days are there in March?

What's the word for more than one mouse?

Questions

Say the number that comes between 23 and 25.

Which word spells a number: f–o–r–e or f–o–u–r?

Julia went to the beach at 2 o'clock and stayed for three hours. What time did she leave?

Which words end with the same letter: "Karl has three apples"?

Answers

8 (or one more)

rain

12

photo and final

Answers

H

a dog

15 (5 + 5 + 5 = 15)

a lamb

Answers

35 and 42

warm, cold

6 (3 + 2 + 1 = 6)

Thursday

Answers

24

f–o–u–r (four)

5 o'clock

has, apples

Answers

a flower

his

31

mice

Answers

60

"This playground doesn't have a slide."

4 (2 + 1 + 1 = 4)

paper (newspaper)

Brainiac Award!

Every time you finish a chapter of this workbook, choose a Brain Quest sticker and place it over the correct square on the certificate below. When all the squares have been covered by stickers, you will have completed the entire Brain Quest Workbook! Woo-hoo! Congratulations! That's quite an achievement.

Once you have a completed certificate, write your name on the line—or use the alphabet stickers—and cut out the award certificate.

Show your friends. Hang it on your wall! You're a certified Brainiac!

Brainiac Award

BRAIN QUEST

Presented to:

_____

for successfully completing all thirteen chapters of

BRAIN QUEST 1ST GRADE WORKBOOK

PLACE A STICKER ON EACH SQUARE AFTER YOU HAVE COMPLETED THE CHAPTER

| Chapter 1 | Chapter 2 | Chapter 3 | Chapter 4 | Chapter 5 | Chapter 6 | Chapter 7 | Chapter 8 | Chapter 9 | Chapter 10 | Chapter 11 | Chapter 12 | Chapter 13 |

It's Fun to Be Smart!®

America's #1 Educational Bestseller, for Pre-K through 7th Grade

Available wherever children's books are sold, or visit brainquest.com.

A A A A A A ★ B B B B

B ★ C C C C C C D D D D

D D D E E E E E E ★ F F

F F ★ G G G G G G G H H

H H H H ★ I I I I I J

J J J J J ★ K K K K K

★ L L L L L L M M M M M

M N N N N N N O O ★ O

O O P P ★ P P P P P Q Q Q

Q Q Q R R R R R ★ S S

S S S ★ T T T T T T T U

U U U U U V ★ V V V V V

W ★ W W W W X X X X X

Y Y Y Y Y Y Z Z Z Z Z